Be Strong > Go On

A STORY OF HOPE

TERRI BAKER-HELTON

Blossom
Book Publishing
A Division of Blossom Marketing & Publishing, LLC

Published by Blossom Book Publishing
Medina, Ohio

Printed in the United States of America

DEDICATION

To all my loved ones who left too soon,
and to everyone who helped guide me in my journey.

CHAPTERS

INTRODUCTION

Terri stared into an empty plastic cup, focusing on the Mickey Mouse face that was smiling back at her. Her blonde curls were sticking to her tear wet face. This tiny four-year-old angel in an oversized T-shirt looked pitiful. The usual arguing and shouting coming from the kitchen made her feel afraid and guilty. Like most kids, Terri was certain that her parents were fighting because of her.

She wondered if mommy and daddy were fighting because she hadn't picked up her toys, or maybe it was because she cried so much. Or maybe it was because she asked so many questions. Whatever the reason, this child was certain she was the reason her parents were so miserable. If only she hadn't asked for that glass of water.

Terri vowed years later, that she would always be on her best behavior so that she could make everyone happy. Her determination somehow made her feel safe.

CHAPTER ONE
The Making of Memories

It seems as though that I don't really have to try to recall the memories of my childhood—they just come. The memories that I do have are never vivid but rather more like patches here and there. One of my favorite memories was playing in my small back yard where there was a glider that was on an old multicolored rusty swing set. I'm sure that I had visited many unusual people and interesting places, but some days, I remember trains going by often, but waiting, wanting them to pick me up, and take me away from the turmoil. Turmoil in a small mind begins to envision things or people to rescue them, like a flying saucer that imaginarily hovered nearby, but was actually an old water tower.

I have a fond memory of the soft, pink flowers that grew in front of our modest house. I can recall my mom arranging them so that they looked like little ladies wearing fancy ballroom dresses with big hoops. At 4-years-old I believed my mom was able to perform magic, especially with what she did with those flowers.

We lived in a little Ohio town called Lodi. Our home was a moderate sized house which was so close to the road that I could feel the mist of water on my face when cars zoomed down the street after it rained. The paint was slowly peeling off our house leaving its white chips laying on the ground, and our dilapidated garage was barely able to stand on its own. There were bushes growing against the screened porch in desperate need of being trimmed with weeds so abundant surrounding them that it was hard to tell the two apart. After all, some weeds are colorful; however, the roses were so vibrant with a fragrance that I could smell them from the open window of my bedroom, and their beauty surrounded the perimeter of our house. They seemed like an oxymoron, but my mother was so proud of these beauties which she planted herself. I also recall a lovely garden in the back of the house with a thinly wired fence that wrapped around it.

1

Within the four walls of my home was its own mixture of thorns and weeds. Daily loud disagreements, the kind that makes a child want to disappear. I would try to focus on my brother, Bryan, when the fights would begin. At a year old, my brother was three years younger than me. He had carrot red hair, freckles, and an immense attitude.

Even at such a young age, I had a big sister sense that made me want to make sure he was okay. As a child I couldn't formulate my thoughts or assess what was going on in my mind as I tried to avoid the storm, let alone my brother. My parents seemed to thrive on bickering, but I was aware of having a deep foreboding sense that perhaps my parents were never going to find common ground or call a truce.

At a time in a child's life that should be filled with laughter and happiness, I have no memory of anything other than shouting and fear. One of my most vivid memories was hearing my mom crying and wailing in her bedroom which was right next to mine. I heard her cursing at my father and calling him things I didn't understand. What I did understand was her telling him to *get out* of our house. He agreed to get out, but first brought his girlfriend to the house when he picked up a few things. I thought that my mother was going to go into a tirade of shouting, but she didn't.

Late, after this incident, I couldn't comprehend all the sudden changes going on in our house. Watching my dad packing his things into boxes and listening to my mom cry as she sat on the couch watching him leave her, made me feel even more uncertain and frightened than the arguing had done. My parents were getting a divorce. My dad finally vacated the house. I didn't understand, of course, but I did feel the sorrow and anguish, and those feelings lasted for quite some time.

A feeling of failure came over me as I watched him drive away. Somehow I believed that this had to be my fault, just like all the arguing had been. That seemed to be the genesis of a lifelong sense of guilt that actually had taken me years to understand.

It's unfortunate that an instruction manual doesn't come with parenthood or marriage because if it had, my parents and a countless number of children would have been spared the grief, and certainly my parents would have been instructed to take the less painful way to explain divorce to their children. The damage they did to me by not explaining what was happening, and by not assuring me that it was not my fault, and that everything would be alright was immeasurable.

It is so important to make sure a child understands that it is not their fault, and to let them know that other families go through the same thing. Parents have a power over their children that they may not even be aware of having. There is unnecessary damage by being careless or there is a strong foundation that comes from intentionally minimizing trauma when traumatic situations occur.

I wish that my parents had kept routines, provided fair discipline, and had set limits. This would have helped my brother and I understand what a family is supposed to be like. Then when arguing occurred we wouldn't have felt so out of place. Holidays, vacations, and other special occasions would have focused on our family.

My parents had few friends to talk to about their relationship with in those days while working and caring for a family. They were not equipped to be parents and certainly didn't focus on the good things in life. One good thing for me and my brother is that our parents didn't say bad things about each other.

Fortunately, I've learned how to deal with a lot of painful changes in my life and as a result I've learned how to be strong and go on. Today I realize that if I could survive verbal abuse, extremely trying situations, and countless daily pressures - anyone can!

CHAPTER TWO
Grandparents

We had spent a lot of time at my grandparents. My maternal grandparents, Florence and Carroll, were positive influences in our life. They were kind, loving and generous people. Too kind in fact, for my future carefree antics as a teen. They watched my brother and me while my mom taught elementary school, worked as a local waitress, and still took classes at Kent State. Like Superwoman, she could leap buildings in a single bound, but also give us hugs and tuck us in at night. I can remember her bending down to softly whisper a goodnight against my cheek while pulling the covers up to my chin. I also remember missing her when she was gone so much trying to better our lives. Regardless of why she was gone – I missed her.

Mom had long dark hair with eyes that changed with her apparel. She was small in size but towering to me. On rare occasions, we were able to accompany her to work at the restaurant. We sat in the back by ourselves with our craft materials, consisting of a box of crayons and some paper. One of the benefits of quietly, waiting patiently was free banana splits. My cantankerous brother never heard of the word patient and obviously did not understand the word patient. I spent most of my precious time chasing the difficult perpetrator, trying to keep him out of trouble. This was an impossible mission. *What are brothers for*, I would think.

Another memory etched in my mind about my brother was on a voyage back from my mother's friend's house. We were perched in the back seat of my mom's small green Mustang. The redheaded wrongdoer looked at me, then proceeded to grab my doll and dangle her out the side window. We began screaming and hitting each other while our mother dished out the idle threats of pulling over and coming back to "straighten us up." After her demands were not met, the car was heading for the median. We quickly put our angelic faces on and had our apologies ready to go. When our patient, kindhearted mother glanced back, she did not look like she was ready for

4

negotiations. As she exited the vehicle, we heard some type of siren in the background that we hoped would save us. My brother and I gazed out the back window where siren noise was coming from. There were bright red and blue lights flashing. Soon, a man wearing a large rim hat that matched his outfit, walked up to our mom. They conversed for a short time while my brother and I wondered what our fate might entail. Then she climbed back in and must have forgot about our conference. Quietness permeated the vehicle, and nothing was said until we arrived home. Then came calm but demanding "Go to bed." The explanation of what the policeman said to her that day was never revealed to us.

Mom was my teacher for about a month in the first grade. My regular teacher was off for maternity leave. All the other kids loved her. They gave her hugs and made pictures for her. I felt so proud and lucky. This was a once in a life time experience which I still feel grateful for today. Besides being a good teacher, she shared her artistic gift with students making Christmas cards with stamps that she etched out of wood, and jewelry that was made from rolled up pieces of magazines. She even made matching outfits for me, my brother and herself to wear when we were out on the town.

Sometimes at night she would teach me easy songs to play on the piano. One time while playing, I fell asleep on the keys with an umbrella on top of my head. Ironically, I had been playing my remake version of "Raindrops Keep Falling on My Head." The *remake* had been because my grandparents owned the old upright player piano which was seriously out of tune, but I loved it anyway.

And then there was my two favorite blankies; they were yellow with silk around the edges. I never went anywhere without at least one of them. One day my mom made the mistake of washing both of them in the same wash, and I needed one of them all the time. I cried and ran out to the clothesline and found the two yellow security friends hanging up soaking wet. So I grabbed onto both of them pulling the corners together, but I couldn't budge them. My arms soon gave out but my determination didn't. I stood there until they were dry enough to take down, even through dinnertime.

My mom finally got her degree from Kent State. She landed a teaching job in New Jersey, and we were on our way. She signed the contract and journeyed out to get us a place to stay. Bryan and I remained back with our grandparents, while my mom and a friend went to start setting up our new life. My mom's friend had two children who stayed with us. During the day I would spend hours meticulously making pictures and cards for my mom's joyous homecoming. I loved to draw. I also liked to make up songs and had a few ballads ready to serenade my mom when she arrived home. While I was designing one of my many "I love you" cards, anticipating her return, there was a knock at the front door.

My grandmother opened the door to see two solemn looking police officers standing on the porch. They looked serious as they quietly spoke to my grandmother. I couldn't decipher what they could possibly be talking about. Then suddenly the gravity of the situation was revealed as my grandmother tearfully turned to me and told me that my mother was never coming home.

No *I love you*, no *goodbyes*, I wanted to hand her my breathtaking pictures and sing to her my love songs. Who was going to put toothpaste on my toothbrush? Who would help me get dressed? Who would put my hair in pigtails? Who would tuck me in at night? My world was over. My mom was it. She had been my whole life—everything. I screamed and cried for hours as my sorrowful grandmother tried to hold me in her arms. I wanted to be left alone. I just didn't understand or believe any of it. The policeman had to be mistaken, confused, whatever, but my life was coming back, I hoped. This couldn't be happening to me - I was only eight. My brother was only five and hadn't even started school yet!

My sweet mother had been killed instantly after being propelled from her small green mustang. According to the police, a young female driver didn't see her coming down the highway and pulled out in front of her. It just didn't seem fathomable to me that this teenage driver's lack of being alert drastically and tragically changed my life forever.

I have always wondered if people knew their time is drawing near. I have heard different stories from people. My mother had given a book to her best friend she had visited on this journey about communicating with the dead. Also, before she left to head back to Ohio, she seemed anxious and kept stating she had to see my brother and me. My aunt gave her blackberries to bring home. My mom said that if they had an accident, there was going to be blackberries all over the road. Well, the blackberries were splattered all over the highway. Her friend that was in the car with my mom sustained serious head injuries but recovered.

I was always confused when people would tell me that I was "lucky to have photos" of my mom. I didn't want her photos back then, I wanted her! But today I realize what they meant and agree with them. I am very fortunate that my parents loved taking photos which are all that I have left today, other than my memories.

I still have the last postcard that my mom sent. It was directly addressed to me. It said, *Here is a picture of the liberty bell. I am staying at Mary Ann's tonight. Saw Nan Brown this morning; See you Tues (probably.) Be good. Love, Mom.* To this day I wish that I understood why she put "probably" in her final postcard to me.

My mom was buried in the eastern part of Ohio, not far from the Pennsylvania border, in the small town where she was born and raised. I don't remember her funeral. My mind draws a blank when I try to recall it. What I do remember is that there wasn't really anyone in my life to console me. No phone calls or visits from well-wishers. Just loneliness. Life just kept moving on as though nothing had happened.

The only thing that I could do was talk to myself and convince myself that I needed to be strong for Bryan and go on with my life the best that I could. My grandma told me that God needed a teacher in heaven which I believed to be the reason she was taken from me. I used that as my source of strength and reasoning. Today I find my comfort in rummaging through my box of keepsakes that hold all of my memories. The photos and cards I had made for my mother; the keys and owner's manual to her 1969 Mustang; her Bachelor of Science in Education degree from Kent State. I love to read the letters that she had written to us and look through her address book and checkbook. Somehow it makes me feel the reality of her – the proof that she existed.

I believe that properly handling a tragic loss in a child's life, such as divorce or the death of a loved one, is the most fundamentally important thing that you can do for the emotional well-being of that child. Talk openly and ask if they have any questions or if they are afraid of anything because in doing so the child will be able to realize their feelings and therefore work through them. Share happy memories, relay beliefs, and if not sure about something admit it. It is still better than saying nothing at all. Reminiscing and missing loved ones is part of the grieving process and important to letting go so that they can move forward.

Another important factor in helping the child move through grief is in keeping routines as much as possible. The boundaries that routines provide can make the child feel a sense of safety. A child should be permitted and encouraged to attend the funeral services or burial ceremony but never forced. Of course the child's age and the circumstances of death need to be considered when making the decision. Prepare them for what to expect at the funeral and what they will see and experience. Explain how people might be crying or even laughing at the service and that this is normal.

Some of the things that helped me as a child were simple activities such as writing poems, songs, or stories on how I was feeling. Making a special photo book of my mother with my grandmothers seemed to really help me deal with my pain. When I was feeling down, I would look at pictures and think of happy times.

My grandparent's plan for retirement went out the window after my mom's death because they wound up taking in me and Bryan full time and raising us since our father didn't want to. He didn't think he could handle it and actually never even offered. So, my loving grandparents took on the role and burden of raising two young children while dealing with their own grief of losing their daughter. My grandma used to tell us that my dad's house was too small to raise us but I know now that was just an excuse. He was too busy being a bachelor.

CHAPTER THREE
The Love of Grandparents

My grandfather was a Quaker nicknamed Red. Rebel Red was his CB handle when he drove a truck. I guess he had red hair at one time. As long as I knew him, it was snow white. Sometimes when I hear the word *Quaker*, I think of the word quiet. But not when it came to Grandpa. He had a kind of thundering disposition and was highly opinionated. I remember more than once when his face turned bright red; his veins protruding from his forehead; and his fists clenching as he proclaimed his point of view. However, he was still a good-natured, kind person that would not hesitate in helping people.

My Quaker grandmother was small in stature, brown, graying hair that was always curled back all around. She too had been very kind, strong-willed, and an inspiration to all. Even though my grandfather's income was menial, they donated time and money to helping others. They volunteered for organizations like Habitat for Humanity, Good Samaritans, the Puritan Club, the Handicap Society; and they served on the county park committee, and wrote to prisoners. They had also volunteered in a program that had city kids from Cleveland come for the summer and stay with families. They found time to visit relatives and to attend family reunions. The twosome were always together and busy. Grandpa and Grandma still had time for my brother and me and as a result they instilled positive qualities of doing good for others in both of us.

I loved living with my grandparents after my mother died. Their home was not large, and was located close to the road and just outside of town. The backyard was my playground. In my imagination it wasn't just a simple back yard. It was a green jungle with big mountains and ravines. I was usually barefoot on my adventures of catching salamanders, skipping rocks, and leading expeditions for the neighbor kids. We built our own forts using any kind of materials that we could sneak out of our houses and garages. These times are warm memories of childhood play and games. I believe that my mother passed on to me her great ability to create with my hands or in my mind. The changing of the Ohio seasons provided countless opportunities to be creative: May Day—flower baskets for neighbors; summer—Kool-Aid stand with club members; and winter—sledding and hot chocolate.

I was a small kid in stature and at school I was a bit quiet and shy. I was a very good student who usually got A's and B's. I was definitely a people-pleaser, which I realized as an adult, and tried to please everybody. I always did what was expected of me.

I enjoyed school with a few exceptions. One thing I disliked was the dreaded *Mother's Day*. Of course, we made things for our moms and I wanted to fit in so I just went along with everyone else in the class, merrily making something that would never be received by the person it was intended for. Even though my multitude of teachers over the years knew that my mom had died, they would normally forget. And so year after year I was faced with the confusing and painful task of pretending that I enjoyed the ritual.

Many of the Mother's Day treasures that I made stayed filed in my flowered book bag which was trimmed in black. I did not like it. Everyone I knew had a mom. Maybe things would have been easier if I had known someone other than myself that was motherless. I felt all alone at times. Also, at this age, children could be unknowingly cruel. I recall being teased a couple of times by the classroom bully who would chant in a cruel way, "I have a mom, and you don't." Unresponsive I would just look down and walk away knowing they were right and feeling that rush of pain that seemed to drown me.

Every school had a bully and my school was no exception. His harsh words lashed out at me as others stared. My bully was tall and lanky. He had straggly blonde reddish hair, and his nose was always trickling snot. I remember a couple of times when he pulled back his fist and punched me in the stomach. I would bend over trying to catch my breath as the bell was blaring for us to come in from recess. He seemed to know when the recess bell was about to ring.

Bent over, holding my stomach, I would slowly make it to the door and return to class while wishing that my teacher would notice the pain that my tormentor was causing. But, just like their lack of awareness over the fact that I was motherless, they were unaware that I was being bullied.

Another non-favorite school day norm for me was the bus ride. On the way to school the bus was always packed and I had to stand and hold on to whatever I could find. I was a frozen target, with an open invitation for spit balls and unwanted items from student's lunches. I would just try to disappear and pretend that I was somewhere else.

One day while I was doing my usual daydreaming, a girl's voice called to me from the back of the bus. She exclaimed that she had saved a seat for me. I wormed my way back to this stranger and stared at her as I sat down next to her. I thanked her quietly. From that day forward I had a place to sit down. At the time she didn't realize what it meant to me. She was nothing more than the girl who saved my seat each day that year on the bus, but to me she was my rescuer. I'm glad that I got the chance to tell her just how much her act of kindness meant to me when I happened to meet her years later, as an adult. I told her how I felt back then and how she gave me something that made a huge difference in the life of a child in pain. She cried as I told her why I was so grateful for her and thanked me for telling her.

It was comforting to me back then that some of my teachers knew my mom. That connection made me feel special. It seemed that those teachers who knew her were extra nice to me, which helped me carry on. Teachers don't always realize what an impact they can have on their student's lives and what an important role they can play in helping them move on from a difficult situation. My fifth grade teacher, Miss Morgan, knew about my loss and went out of her way to help me. She would take me, along with a few other girls, on fun excursions after school. These getaways never failed to make me forget about my painful life and offer a moment of much needed reprieve.

My brother, on the other hand, could not find any good point to school.

Teachers didn't have the time or patience with him that they should have had. His strong will and controversial attitude made it tough for him at school. He really struggled with learning and obeying rules. Sometimes, when they would let him out for recess, he would skip school. Even at the age of seven, he would slide through the fence, cut through the woods, and like a hound dog, would somehow find his way home. My grandmother would call the school to let them know of his arrival.

With his anger and short attention span problems, it was hard for him to do anything. One extraordinary feat that I do remember him accomplishing was that he heard a song only once, and he was able to play it on the piano. On one of our many trips, we visited Stephen Foster's home. When we got back, he could play "I Dream of Jeannie with the Light Brown Hair" and "Camp town Races", with no problem. I am sure he had many other hidden talents too but he never had the patience to uncover them.

Like any child, Christmas was the one time of the year where it was easier to be happy, even though I knew my Christmas wish of having my mom back could never come true. One of my faithful friends around this time of year was our single copy of the Sears and Roebuck *Wish Book* which we reused over and over. I looked at the catalog all year in anticipation of the coming Christmas. It's torn and worn pages showed its use. There was a pink Cadillac pedal car in the catalog that I had wished for until I was too grown up to have it.

The Christmas ambiance at grandma's house was cheery and I would get excited as relatives arrived. I especially remember my Aunt June who was like Santa to me. She usually arrived late in the evening, laying on her horn a mile down the road. Her small car would be packed to maximum capacity with wrapped presents for everyone. She made Christmas, birthdays, and every holiday more special. With her notes, cards, presents, and phone calls, she remained faithful to us and impacted my life in immeasurable ways.

The Christmas after my mom passed away, I would hide in her closet to be closer to her. I would hug her clothes and any of her belongings that I could find stored away in boxes. I would look at pictures that she had drawn, items she had once hung up in her classrooms, and fan mail students had written to her. One day, while I was hidden away, I saw some unusual colored papers tucked under an old heavy quilt. As I pulled it aside, I noticed that there were three brightly wrapped packages. I grinned, grabbed the box, and ran downstairs to share my find with everybody. I couldn't locate my brother, so I turned to my grandmother. She was easy to find with the smell of fresh bread coming from the kitchen. She inspected the treasures and said one might be mine, and the other two were for my brother. She said that she didn't know anything about them. We put them under the tree and decided to wait until Christmas to do the unwrapping. It meant a lot to receive one more gift from my mother. Something she touched and wrapped herself.

On Christmas morning I ripped open the box with brightly colored wrapping paper and found a doll that I had seen in my favorite picture book. It was a Little Kiddle doll that I had wanted. It was one of those special gifts that a little girl had to have. I clung to this doll like no other and spent years loving her. My brother got a drum and an Indian headdress with brightly colored feathers. We constantly heard the drum for a long time after that Christmas day.

My grandmother did many things over the years for my brother and me. One was a journal she kept containing our funny quips and quirks when we were younger. My favorite picture to this day had been taken when I was four years old standing on a scale. The quip: *Does it weighs my tummy or my feet?* My favorite quip from my brother was; *all flies were his friends.*

My grandmother had her hands full with us. She would try to keep us busy with different crafts and toys she had made. We were fascinated with a marble rack she had made, a jumping jack monkey, and a spinning button on a string. She was so creative that she made us a set of blocks made from wooden spools. Grandma would cut fashion models out from magazines and paper clothes to dress them with. She was as devoted as a grandmother could be.

She was also a great rescuer and warrior when it came to bats. Whenever she would hear our screams of horror from upstairs, she usually knew what the culprit was. With her weapons in hand—a broom and a paper bag—she would climb up the steps to conquer and dispose of the evil *flitter mouse*. One time she needed my assistance and asked me to hold the bag. I crouched under her flowered bathrobe, because I didn't want it to get in my hair, and waved the trap from side to side. She must have whacked the fierce predator with the broom pretty hard because it was nowhere in sight. After we made her check every nook and cranny, she said a goodnight and went back downstairs. I climbed back up to the top of the bunk bed and tried to fall asleep.

The next day no more thoughts were given to the bat. We were enjoying the day outside and making up more adventures. Grandma was sweeping the front porch and told us she was going in because her pants were bothering her. Not thinking much of that statement, we kept collecting intriguing bugs to put in a glass jar. Then she strolled back out and nonchalantly told us she found the bat—in her pants. Any normal person would have been screaming about that. No matter what the predicament might be, grandma was cool, calm, and collected.

If there was one thing for certain about my grandmother it was that she was never too exhausted to make us feel special. She made us a portfolio of our artwork that we had created over the years. I still have mine today. There was also never a missed opportunity to make special occasions seem spectacular, especially birthdays. She always tried to make our birthdays be the best they could be. She would bake her traditional heart-shaped cake which I adored especially since my birthday was in February, just before Valentine's Day.

My dad's mom lived in a big old white farmhouse on a country road on the other side of town. I remember her making us big ole' left over pot roast sandwiches to snack on before going to bed. She was a very kind, loving person.

15

CHAPTER FOUR
Influences and Challenges

I've come to understand over the years that there is a depravity in the minds of some that seek out the fulfillment of their own needs, regardless of how heinous or devastating. As a blight on society, pedophiles lurk around the most vulnerable of victims. Regardless of the loss and sadness in my life caused from losing my mother, I was no exception to the perverted compulsion of a man I trusted.

One unfortunate memory hidden far back in the recesses of my mind is the experience of being robbed of my innocence by a trusted family friend who just so happened to be a pedophile. He would come over to visit and make everyone believe that he was kind, jovial and trustworthy. Cunningly, he would play a game with me that he called *Tickle,* whenever he would get me alone. What was so confusing to me is that he referred to it as a game. If it was a game, why did it make me feel so yucky and why couldn't I tell anyone?

It didn't matter where we were. He was touching my body in places that I did not want him to touch. He was doing things to me that did not feel right and that I did not like. After convincing myself that "games" shouldn't feel so ugly, I got up the courage to say, "NO!" I told him that I was going to tell if he didn't leave me alone. Because of my basically shy and timid nature, it took everything in me to tell him to leave me alone. I didn't realize my own courage until that very moment and the knowledge and empowerment I felt has never left me. After telling him, I would do my best to stay totally away from him.

By the age of eleven, I started thinking, *Why me?* I began questioning everything in my life which soon led to resentment. Not understanding what I was feeling or why, I began to take things out on my grandma. She deserved hugs and praises but instead I showered her with my moodiness and rebellion. I found myself hating everything in my life, especially the layers and layers of tattered quilts and blankets that I had to lay under in order to stay warm since we had no heat upstairs where my bedroom was. I wanted the whole world to leave me alone.

Sixth grade was especially difficult. I missed as many days as I attended and my grandparents didn't have a clue on how to deal with me. They tried to guide me and offer help but I did not want to listen. So, one day my school principal came knocking on my bedroom door. He strolled right on into my pit of gloomy despair. Despite my messy room and bad attitude, he sat down on the end of my bed. He gave the normal pep-talk while pointing out the good things to look at in life. We conversed a little while, and then he headed back to school.

After he had left, I threw my wood-grain music alarm clock across the room and thought about what he said. Then I got up and dug my cherished clock out of a pile of dirty clothes and plugged it back into the one and only outlet in my room. I tuned into static and found my favorite station. I loved music, it helped me through so much in life. I let myself get lost in the music after I thought about the wisdom that Mr. Bangert tried to bestow upon me.

Even though I missed a lot of school, I still received good grades and awards in music and art. I was fortunate to have a caring principal and supporting teachers which played a big part in my success at school. On the home front, I was in a little bit better spirits since my impromptu pep-talk. I was no longer howling at my grandmother and was helping around the house more.

I went back into the fray of things, working on my grades, attitude, and my disposition to others. My special grandmother tried to keep everything going as smoothly as possible, and keeping us as happy as possible. She would sing my favorite song that was about a goat eating red long johns off the clothesline, which saved him from being hit by a train. She read us bedtime stories, and helped us feel good about ourselves. She was such an important influence in my life, and everything seemed to be going better.

One good thing during this time was that I got the chance to get to know my father. He came to my grandparents at least every other weekend. He would stop in during the week to just say "Hi." My dad was not very tall. He had dark hair and a mustache; and sometimes wore a beard. He typically wore jeans with a flannel or button-up dress shirt.

I always looked forward to his visits. I'd anticipate him coming and looked forward to his hugs. I remember dashing out the front door whenever my dad's big blue car would pull in the driveway. When we got a little older, there would be times that he would pick us up, and we would go for a ride. A ride consisted of driving around to nowhere in particular and singing the entire time. We did a lot of singing. When I think of these days, I think of music and laughter. My dad could always make me laugh with his silly stories, jokes, and faces. His sense of humor was one of the things that I loved most about him. He taught me to be able to laugh especially when frivolous worries were piling up.

Bryan and me would go to the park with our dad and play for hours on end. Sometimes my dad would kick back and fall asleep on the bench as we played leap frog over him or covered him up with leaves. We'd also go fishing which was one of my dad's favorite things to do. We had our very own poles that he kept in the trunk of his car. I didn't always understand all of the waiting and the time consuming sitting that went along with fishing, but I was happy to do anything with my dad.

We went to the movies a lot. There was a little theater in our town that played movies that had been out for a while. It was even fun going to the laundry mat to wash his clothes. It didn't matter what we were doing, it was awesome and I was happy. It felt like celebrating a birthday because whenever he took us to the local grocery store, he would let us pick out any type of candy. While we browsed the candy aisle, he would be picking out his cigars or his cherry smelling tobacco for his pipe. Then we would head to his bachelor pad. He really didn't have very much; a broken brown recliner in the corner, a velvet flower couch along the wall, and a TV that played fuzzy pictures. I also recall wire black chairs with a metal table, and plastic colored flowers that served as a centerpiece. He had a broken toaster and dishes that didn't match which were always sitting in the kitchen sink waiting to be washed. Compared to the tiny place he lived in before, this apartment was a palace. It had a walk in kitchen and a bedroom off the living room. Best of all, it was right around the corner from my grandparents house.

Whenever we would visit my dad, we always seemed to play a game he called "Who can be the quietest?" Dad would always end up winning.

I specifically remember one particular visit with my dad as we were cruising around town. He asked me what I would want if I could have anything at all. Most twelve-year-olds may have had a hard time deciding what they would want, but not me. I knew exactly what I wanted because I had wanted it for so long. I just smiled at my dad without saying a word because I knew that he knew the answer to the question. We both just smiled.

We drove to his apartment and when we arrived he told me to check out the bedroom closet. I ran into his apartment as fast as I could and rushed to the closet. All I saw was his shirts hanging neatly in a row. He told me to look toward the back, behind the shirts. There it was. Hidden carefully behind a striped sheet was the very thing I had wanted, dreamed of and imagined holding in my arms. A beautiful electric guitar! It also had an amplifier which only made this perfect gift even more perfect. My first thought when I saw this incredible gift was that now my dad and I could jam and sing together. When I looked over at him to exclaim my absolute joy, he was wiping his eyes. He was happy to see me happy.

I've only seen my dad cry one other time which was at my mom's funeral. He told me how much he loved her and how badly he was going to miss her. It felt strange yet comforting at the same time when he held me and cried. I knew in that moment that he loved her regardless of their divorce. And now, seeing him get teary over seeing my joy over the guitar, I knew how much he loved me.

Over the years I got to meet many of my dad's girlfriends. Some would go out of their way to show how much they cared about me and Bryan so that they would be accepted by my dad, and some were blatant about how much they didn't want my brother and me around.

I remember one of his girlfriends who seemed to genuinely care about us. She treated us like we were her children. She would play games with us, read books with us, and make us laugh. One time she took us sledding at a golf course while my dad was sleeping. I thought this was so cool. I felt myself starting to really like her but at the same time felt uneasy. I didn't want to get hurt and I knew how many girlfriends my dad had over the years. And, just as I feared, things came to an abrupt end one day and I never saw her again. Nothing more was said about her, and I didn't want to ask. As long as my dad was around, and he kept picking us up, I would adjust. I just loved any time I got to spend with him.

CHAPTER FIVE
Teenage Trials and Tragedy

At the age of fourteen I entered Jr. High, and like most teens, I had a chip on my shoulder. I also thought that I knew everything that I would ever need to know. I think my "take-a-hike" attitude was part of the reason that I frequently got into situations at school that wound up with someone wanting to kick my butt.

I tried very hard to fit in and worked at making new friends which I eventually did. I found that many of the friends that I made during this time needed occasional encouragement and support. Whether it was problems with their boyfriends, parents, or school work, they talked to me about it. What I discovered about myself is that my many years of dealing with the pain of loss in my life, and the challenges that occur when you are motherless from a young age, seemed to give me a wisdom about life that the average teen lacked. I drew from my own experiences which turned out to be helpful to my friends. So, my role amongst my friends seemed to be that of guidance counselor.

My life certainly didn't look anything like the TV families or the other families that seemed *normal* to me, so I just walked around feeling abnormal. I didn't feel like I had anybody I could talk to. Sometimes my world looked very bleak. That must be why I gravitated towards boys who made me feel alive and wanted which is a pretty dangerous combination.

Eric and Jimmy were two guys that I went to school with. Jimmy asked me if I wanted to take a ride with him and Eric. They were cute and I didn't have anything better to do so I agreed to go. *Why not? What could it hurt?* Eric gestured for me to get in the back with him and lifted his seat up for me to join him. I squeezed in and away we went. It seemed pretty neat to me with the music blaring and the boys flirting with me. What more could a teen ask for? Well, our adventure did not last long. Almost simultaneously to noticing that Jimmy was driving really fast and his speedometer was climbing, we slammed into a telephone pole. My body smashed into the back of his seat and then I jolted backwards. I held my head and glanced over at the Eric. His nose appeared to be severed from his face and blood was splattered everywhere. I looked over towards Jimmy who was gone. His body had been launched through the windshield.

I crawled out of the wreckage and saw that Jimmy was barely conscious. I noticed that his front teeth were gone and blood was profusely pouring from his face. The screaming that was coming from him was deafening and I wasn't sure what to do. I yelled out to him that I was going for help. I started running toward an old farmhouse and could feel my heart pounding in my chest. This seemed so surreal but the cries of my friends reminded me of the reality of the moment.

I ran up the front steps of the house and pounded on the door. A startled old lady slowly opened the door and I quickly began to explain what happened before she shut the door. I'm sure that the look on my face, and my trembling, blood covered hands told her that she needed to help me. In a shaky voice, she told me to wait there as she scurried off. She came back quickly and handed me a blanket to wrap up in and told me that she called for an ambulance.

I thanked her for the blanket as I jumped off the porch explaining that I needed to get back to my friends. By the time I got back to the car, I could hear sirens in the distance and felt a lot of relief. Jimmy was still laying in the field groaning. Eric was crying and rocking back and forth with his head hung between his legs.

Two ambulances and several police cars surrounded us and began to work quickly on my friends. Once they were loaded into the ambulances, the policeman who arrived first began to question me about what happened. I wasn't very much help since I only knew Jimmy and Eric's first names. I wasn't willing to admit that Jimmy was speeding and spoke very cautiously. The cop could see that I was shaken and stopped questioning me. He gave me a ride home.

Sadly, I found out the next day that Jimmy died. Hearing the news made me feel a myriad of emotions – recalling how it felt when I got the tragic news of my mother's death while simultaneously making me overwhelmingly grateful that my life had been spared. I whispered to my mom, *thank you for protecting me,* feeling confident she had something to do with it.

I now had another experience to add to my life's repertoire and wouldn't hesitate to advise my friends on the importance of driving responsibly.

Trying to put the tragedy behind me, I immersed myself in music – my reprieve from most everything. I especially loved playing my mom's 45's and albums on our old record player. Whenever I got any money, I would save it up to buy albums. My first 45 was "With a Little Luck." I would blare that song and sing on the top of my lungs using anything that I could find as a makeshift mic, including spoons, brushes and screwdrivers. I also spent hours dancing to my favorite tunes.

When I wasn't making music I was usually getting into trouble. Instead of working on my schoolwork, I was working on my social calendar which was far more important to me at that time than good grades. I found myself hanging out more with my rebel friends and hating any authoritative adult. Sometimes I would sneak out in the middle of the night and wander off.

At fourteen, I thought that I could do whatever I wanted. My friends and I would think up little excursions and go there. Like running around the police station at midnight, which doesn't sound too bad, but we only had underwear and high heels on. I remember carving "Unite Pickle Power" in big letters on an apartment building sign and then we hid behind some prickly bushes singing "Jolean the Pickle Queen." A hit I created with a friend, inspired by a pickle. We made up songs about anything. We were able to make our own fun and spent most of our time laughing. As teens, we always had a supply of toilet paper and carried a bar of soap in our back pocket.

My grandparents were always taking trips. Sometimes we were lucky enough to go with them. Otherwise, we stayed with relatives. They always owned a camper. The first type was a pickup with a camper. The only problem with that is that they didn't get to find out about knock down, knock out brawls between my brother and me until we reached rest areas. So they installed an intercom system; however, that only made it so they could hear the knock down, knock out fights. It wasn't long after that that they got an RV, so they could referee and stop any fighting. I visited at least 32 states. Of course, back then I did not appreciate it like I should have. I was very fortunate. I got a chance to see a lot of interesting places.

One of the times my grandparents were able to take a vacation from my brother and me, and an aunt and uncle stayed with us. They had grounded me for one bad action or another. I just wasn't a good listener. I talked to my dad into picking me up and telling my aunt and uncle he needed me to babysit. I wanted out of the restrictive household. It was my birthday Monday anyway. My world evolved around me. My dad came and took me to my favorite teenage hangout. Local celebrities, Big Chuck and Little John, were going to be there. I just had to meet them. They hosted late night movies on Friday in our area. It was a big deal if you were lucky or able to stay up that late and watch them. I remember a few times at slumber parties making it almost to the end of the show before falling asleep. A teen was *famous* if she made it to the end, and then she didn't get shaving cream in her hand either.

My dad said, "Happy Birthday", as I exited the vehicle. He also told me to tell Lil John, he looked like John Wayne. We said a goodbye and away I went. I strolled in with my eminent attitude that I seemed to carry with me wherever I went. I spotted some of my friends and sat down at their table. We did our usual gossiping, put three times as much cherry lip gloss on, as needed, and doused our hair with spray. We would occasionally break out randomly in a song and dance which made us feel so cool. But when we wanted to look really cool we visited the smoking room. This was a talent I would try to acquire but could not figure out the inhaling part. So I would just sit there with this small white stick between my fingers waving it as I talked and pretended I was just as cool as everyone else was.

I would always look for this one guy I had met there. The kind that had a bright light shining over his head like a spotlight, his hair was never out of place; he could blow bubbles from under his tongue, and had a killer southern accent. He was nowhere in sight, so I was plotting the right time to meet the real stars. When the fans started to die down, I marched right up to Lil' John and told him what my dad declared. He laughed, I shook their hands, and it was time for them to go. Not too long after that, I looked up and saw my dad standing in the doorway. He called me over and said we had to leave. My dad seemed a little different, but I couldn't put my finger on it. I said goodbye to everyone, and we went on our way.

We got into the vehicle as my dad told me that he wanted me to meet someone. He took me to the place where he waited. This place was huge and I nervously walked in with him. I was still trying to figure out what was up my dad because he seemed so different. I walked in and saw Lil' John sitting at a table. We walked over and my dad told him he looked like John Wayne. Lil' John laughed.

My dad drank and talked with a few people. By this point, I was worn out and told my dad that I was heading out to the car. My dad said "okay," and told me that he'd be out soon. I remember it being cold as I hiked out to the vehicle. I got in and used my long winter coat to huddle up in. As soon as I was settled, there was a knock on the window. I rolled the window down to see John Wayne's twin. He offered a ride to my dad and me. He wanted to make sure we got home safely, and said my father really shouldn't be driving. I guess I just couldn't comprehend that concept. Of course, he is able to drive, he drives every day, besides that, he's invincible.

I told him thanks, but we would be fine. I had just laid back down when the driver's door swung open. My dad got in I could tell he had been crying. I asked him what was wrong. He stammered out that he missed my mom and told me how much he loved her. Then he started the big blue full size car, and we made our way out of the obstacle ridden parking lot. We had not made it very far before we pulled into a factory parking lot. He abruptly stopped the car, glared at me, and asked if I could drive. I thought he was kidding. I didn't have a clue. I was almost fifteen but I had not read that book yet. I wished I was more knowledgeable about driving, about drinking, about combining the two. In my eyes, dad could do no wrong and was immortal.

Back to my distressing adventure. He looked away, backed the car up, and we started out again. At one time, we were very close to home. I had seen a familiar house, and we pulled into the long gravel driveway. I was hoping and praying to see someone, anyone, that could give my dad some back up. Instead, he turned the car around, and headed right back toward the town that we had just left. I tried telling him to no avail, he said he knew what he was doing. I had such a helpless, powerless, hopeless feeling inside.

I remember "Blinded by the Light" was blaring on the radio. We started picking up speed, and plowed into a car, ran over a stop sign, and then came to a forceful halt. It was all very blurry. Then I looked over at my dad, and he was slumped over the steering wheel; his right arm on my lap. My legs were pinned under the seat, pushed way under by the whole front end of the car. All of a sudden it seemed lights out, and a soft distant voice stated my name. It told me to put my head down. Hearing my name kind of made me coherent, maybe it was a guardian angel. Otherwise, I probably would have had a face full of glass. Then I remember people using some kind of mechanical device to pry me out of the wreckage. My dad must have foreseen what was going to happen, and quickly used his arm to try and hold me back. At that time seat belts were optional. I'm not sure if my dad hit the gas pedal instead of the brake when we were coming to the stop sign or what. I found out later, we were traveling at a very high rate of speed.

The next thing I remember, I was laying down looking up at people. I thought in my mind that I would not ask about my dad's condition, because I knew the news would not be good. Later I heard someone saying that I kept asking where my dad was. The doctor looked down at me and said my dad did not make it. I said nothing, I don't think I even blinked an eye. He repeated it again, I said, "I know." I think they were expecting me to scream, cry, or something, but I just lay there, lifeless inside. I just wanted everyone to stop looking at me. I wanted to go back to hiding under my tattered quilts.

I was in stable condition. I crushed and broke a few bones, and was going to be laid up for a while. I was lucky that I wasn't thrown through the windshield. One thing that I do with everything in life is look for the good. Find the things I am thankful for, because there are so many. It makes it easier if I look for the good and don't dwell on the bad. If I sit around and feel sorry for myself, or just dwell on the negative too long, I will soon be sitting by myself. Any challenge I am confronted with, I draw inner strength and courage and go on. I believed that my mission on this planet must not be completed yet.

They let me out of the hospital on my birthday to go to my dad's funeral. Happy Birthday to me I had thought. I was wheeled in, made it to the first archway, and it seemed like everyone turned and stared at me. It was all probably in my head, but I could not make the long journey down the walkway to the casket. I just wanted to go home and find my quilts, so they steered me out. My dad had a lot of friends there. I know I lost my best friend—goodbye my hero.

Maybe God needed a welder up there, because he was very good. He was one of the supervisors at work. I believe that when it is your time, then it is your time. No matter what age you might be. There is no reason to spend the rest of your eternal life looking for answers and dwelling on *why?* It can consume all the energy and will that I have, and make me forget myself and others around me, who need and care about me. Life goes on. I know that to there is a reason and a purpose for everything. I also believe God listens and answers prayers wherever I may be. I don't have to be standing in an elaborate structure like a church. You can be in the woods, a car, on the ocean, on a mountain, it doesn't matter, and He hears me. I now attempt to think before doing, and remember I am never alone.

After the funeral, I was able to talk to my dad's mom. She told me about a fortune-teller that she had gone to see. The soothsayer told her that one of her sons would die unexpectedly. He would be drinking and driving and taking his daughter home. My grandmother thought that if this horrible fate was going to occur, it would be one of her other sons, but not my father. She also went on to tell me about a blackbird that entered her house the night before the accident. She believed that meant death.

My dad always had a smile on his face. He was always laughing and telling jokes. I laid in my makeshift bed in the living room thinking of him. I actually had too much *why me?* time again. I am better if I keep busy doing something, especially if I am able to help someone. There really wasn't much I could do. I decided to work on my appearance. I sat up looked in a mirror, and tried to put makeup on my puffy face. I thought that maybe if I looked better, I would feel better, but nothing helped my big swollen, black-eyes. I went back to hiding under my covers. I did a lot of sleeping, dreaming, and reviewing memories. I regressed back to my creative side and my lost imagination. I wrote letters to friends and drew pictures of our escapades we had. To my closest friend, I recorded a one-hundred and five page memorandum. Using front and back of my note book paper. When my hand was extremely tired, I took a break. That was the only working limb I had, so I had to use it conservatively. I laid back down and stared at the ceiling.

In this life, on this plain I don't always get a second chance to tell someone how much I care and love them. I understand and believe they *know* that in the world after, how much I cared, but why let this time on earth lie in limbo? Now, I just get to look back in time, and wished I would have told my mom or dad that I loved them more. Everyone knows how much they mean to me, and I try to never take anyone for granted. They could be gone in a blink of an eye. Life is so short.

One day, I asked someone to bring down my trusty radio alarm clock from my room. I turned it on and closed my eyes. Music brought me down to earth. As I regressed, different songs had different meanings to me and brought back special memories. They were times I got to spend with my hero. I could see him sitting in the driver's seat singing and laughing. It was like his way of communicating to me. To this day, like clockwork, if I am feeling down or lonely I can turn the radio on and 'Blinded by the Light' will be on. It reminds me of day I lost my best friend, but that aspiring tune also lets me know that he is thinking of me.

Songs helped me get through the healing process, mentally, and physically. Again, I was reminded that I had pictures of him to look at. When I was able to move around more and get into a wheel chair, I was permitted to have a tutor come to the house. It was time to buck up, be strong, and go on.

The tutor that came to my grandmother's house stopped full time teaching not too long ago at our local junior high. He helped me out so much. Not only in all the basic subjects, but he told me jokes and made me laugh. Something I feel at that time of my life, I needed more than English or History. I can't even imagine not being able to laugh or smile. He helped me get my grades back on track. Before the accident they were on a steady downhill spiral. It gave me hope and a fresh start with school. I finally graduated to a walker and then to crutches. I was able to return to school. Almost all the teachers gave me the encouragement that I had needed in order to go on. I feel sorry for the teachers who can't look past the subject they are teaching and give a little compassion to a student when they need it in their lives. I understand, especially in today's world, more than ever people have to be careful of crossing boundaries. That is sad, because a pat on the back, or a *great job* goes along way, when everything is not going the way I wish that it would in my life. I finished the school year, and was on my way to recovery.

CHAPTER SIX
My Adventures On the Jersey Shore

That summer my relatives thought it would be good for me to start the next year in a new environment, with new people. So my brother and I moved to an aunt and uncle's house in New Jersey. Instead of fighting and grasping onto a lot of negative energy, I was beginning to open up to new ventures. It's easier to be flexible in life with any changing circumstances. I know staying with my grandparents had to be rough on them. We were both, especially my brother, very unpredictable, one day, fine and the next day grouchy. This understandable with all the misfortune thrown our way so early in life. There were so many frustrations, feelings and changes that were hard to deal with. I'm sure my grandparents needed to breathe. They had busy schedules, and loved to travel, too.

At any age it is hard to start over, meet people, and fit in, especially a teenager. We left everything behind we had been familiar with, good or bad. I was fifteen and my brother was twelve. It was not like everyone in our new town had his or her arms wide open and wanted to give us a hug, and tell us that everything will be okay. Yet, that's what I needed. Everybody needs that. If there had been a job position in this area, I would take it. I would be great at it. I would assure everyone tomorrow would come, and it would be better. When a change or move is in a child's future, I would help prepare them; answer questions, and give any positive effects in the move. Whether the teen needs more room to engage in recreation, more friends to make, or just to have a pet gerbil. Finding places teens would like nearby, visiting the school they will be attending, or go for a walk in the new neighborhood. Make sure the teen knows that they can still keep in contact with old friends and family.

In New Jersey, everyone already had his or her own friends and own cliques. I was a total outsider trying to get in. People would ask me about my strange accent, and I used this as a conversation tool. Sometimes my photography teacher would have me stand in front of the class and say philosophical words or answer pertinent questions. Like, say the word roof, potato, or creek. They were amazed a soda was a pop, and I was amazed that a pizza was actually a pie. As long as I knew the jargon, I talked normal, and they were the ones with a drawl. I carried on the charade. I used this ploy to move in, infiltrate a couple of cliques, and met some people. This state has some very friendly people, especially after they know for sure you're not a *bennie.* (Someone not just vacationing)

One of the first people who spoke to me was at my bus stop. I believe it was fate. She told me that my shoe string was untied, and the conversation just flowed. She was going to need someone to help her through some rough times ahead, and I believed that was me. Her name was Debbie. She was different, kind of quiet, but she had her opinions. Her eyes were icy blue, she had long brown hair, and her cheeks were always red. It seemed like it didn't take long, and we could solve the world's problems. She lived on the next street over from me. She was always at my house, or I was at hers. We did a lot together. She introduced me to the Pebble Beach Gang. They were all unique in their own little way. Different shapes, sizes, personalities, and beliefs. Boy, they were a motley crew. I had to have a good pair of tennis shoes, because these people did a lot of walking. They were good talkers and major dreamers too.

My new friend's parents had divorced a few years earlier. She lived with her dad. Debbie was the youngest, her brothers and sisters seemed a lot older than she was and lived elsewhere. I never got to meet her mom. It wasn't long after I met my new found friend, an older sister dropped in while I was there. She was crying and pulled my friend to the side. She told her that their mom had passed away. She had cancer. There were no *I love you* or *goodbyes.* We hadn't known each other for long, but she asked if I would go to the funeral. We talked and talked, and stayed up all night. I knew the awful, lonely state all too well. She was just older then I when her mother past on. I helped her move on the best I could. Matter of fact, we did a lot

31

of walking. We rarely had a destination either. We were *cruising*, minus the car. We were totally together when I got a blue portable 8-track player that followed us wherever we went. We always had music on our escapades. We would play them over and over until the tape would break. We went through a lot of 8-tracks. (Did you ever try and carry those things in your pocket?)

At times, I remember our brain being on pause. One of those times in particular, we had walked pretty far and our legs were getting tired, and soon we put our thumbs out. I wish we had taken our shoes off, pulled our hair out, even stuck our tongues out, but not our thumbs. It didn't take long, an older rusty brown colored car pulled up. We opened the door and we both glanced in. He seemed like your every day normal person. So we both jumped in the front seat and declared our destination. We started conversing, then all of a sudden our simple conversation took an awful turn. The normal looking human started telling us how he was going to chop up our dead bodies, and how he would dispose of our corpses. I felt like I might have been in a bad dream or something. I wanted to wake up or jump out. I casually looked down at the side of the door and saw no door handle. *Okay, don't panic,* I thought. I nudged my horrified pale faced friend and used my eyes to point out the no door handle situation. The guy kept reviewing our horrible fate as he drove past the exit we wanted. My friend and I held hands as I felt my body go numb. I stared straight ahead as he veered off the following exit. He pulled into a restaurant parking lot and hastily stopped the car. Our bodies paralyzed as we watched him get out of the car and run over to our door. He jerked it open and demanded we get out. We slowly edged out as we went over our ill-gotten fate in our minds. He then pointed toward a pay phone and told us to call someone to pick us up, as he handed us a hand full of change. He then proclaimed if he ever saw us hitchhiking again, he *would* kill us. As we staggered our limp bodies to the phone, he proceeded to tell us about his younger sister being raped and killed by someone after accepting a ride. So his crusade in life was to go and look for young people and scare the crap out of them. As we approached the phone, the man walked back to his vehicle and sped away, as my friend and I were just trying to breathe.

All right, so the lesson to be learned is, don't accept rides from strangers, well read on. A bunch of our gang was going to Seaside Heights, the boardwalk nearby. We all rode in different vehicles. We got a ride from Debbie's friend's brother, and a neighbor's cousin. We crowded into his shiny new pickup that was only equipped with a front seat. There was no intense conversation on the way, just your every day normal small talk. When we all arrived, we went our own separate ways. We did our customary walking ritual up and down the boardwalk. Every once in a while, we would stop and play pinball or skeet ball until our funds were tired of it. It was getting dark so we started looking for the others. We finally ran into the two guys who brought us. It was easy to see the neighbor's cousin had been drinking, and he offered us different types of drugs. We responded with a "NO," and turned back to the driver and inquired about a ride home. He said sure, and he seemed fine. We walked to the truck and crammed in. Debbie stumbled. We all talked a little. I was anticipating the arrival home and jumping into bed, my legs were very tired. Then out of a nowhere the neighbor's cousin blurted out that he just got out of prison and proceeded to talk about his adventures there. As he tried to swoon us about his romantic myths, he started rubbing my leg, I kept taking his hand off. This went on until I looked into his dreamy dilated pupils and yelled, "stop it!' He then ordered his friend to pull off to the side of the road. The guy driving changed the conversation and kept trying to get us home safely. Then the maniac passenger to my right started screaming to our driver he was going to kill us all if he did not pull the bleeping truck over. After that he informed me that I had been leading him on the entire voyage. This outrageous, idiotic statement left me speechless. The madman pointed and commanded the driver to pull into a sandy drive. It was hidden by a bunch of pine trees. As we pulled back into this desolated area, we begged and pleaded for him to just keep driving us home. We tried to calm down the maniac, but he said he was on a mission to teach me a lesson. Suddenly my friend's brother shut the vehicle off and went limp. He looked like he was playing possum, or something. Next thing I know, the lunatic opens the door and clutched onto my arm. My girlfriend grasped onto me and both of us held onto the steering wheel for dear life. He kept trying to pull me out of the truck. We screamed at the driver for help, but he was just sitting in pause. So, it was up to my friend and me to escape the trenches of this evil villain. After struggling, it seemed like hours, he let go and ran off into the dark pine trees. We both were trying to catch our breath and convince the driver to take off. When an arm came in and yanked me to the pine-filled ground. The villain jumped on top of me, sitting on me as he ripped the buttons off my shirt. Debbie's small frame pounced on his back, hitting and punching his head. He yanked her off by pulling her long brown hair, right to the ground. As he got off of me to attack my friend, he called us both unflattering names. We both leaped up and together shoved him down. We started to run and he snatched Debbie's ankle, yanking her back to the ground. As I tried to help her up, he clutched me by my hair. We both were screaming and kicking. Finally one of us must have got him in the right spot. He let go of my hair as he lunged forward holding onto the front of himself. He went down to the ground. How did I get back into a bad dream? Debbie and I just started running in the complete blackness. We held hands and headed toward some light. My legs felt numb, but we made it to a street light. I was out of breath, I just wanted to drop, but we kept on running, as we tried to figure out where we were. We finally recognized some houses and street names, and made it home. I was over an hour late and definitely grounded for that one.

No more accepting rides from strangers, almost strangers, or anyone we're not sure about. I advise it even more strongly in today's world. I won't do it. I listen to the little voice in my head. If I don't hear it, I turn it up. In anything I plan in life, I think first. Just like drugs – which I don't do now. They are so far from being cool. This is advice from someone who knows firsthand. I had always hated getting advice or lectures from people who were clueless about the subject they were talking about. Especially as a teenager, because at that time I knew everything about anything. There are no happy positive possibilities in using drugs. The negative effects outweigh them tremendously. My outlook on life: things that happen that affect people around me, do not necessarily effect me. Around drugs, it's hard to decipher real friends, and people who really care about what me and what happens to me. Life is twice as blurry.

When a person is addicted to a problem, people who don't understand the disease usually look or talk down to that person, or end up walking away in total disgust. Some people linger in denial. Doing drugs might seem fun or exciting, but slowly it turns into a very lonely ordeal or eventually death. I have lost a lot of good friends for no reason. I have seen friends lose any one thing and everything that meant anything to them. Friends of mine have died from drug deals gone bad, overdosed, killed for their drugs, or have killed themselves because of the endless, hopeless feeling of losing everything they had. I have not experienced or seen anything good coming from drugs—in the end. If someone offers drugs say, "NO," and walk away. Telling someone that I'm high on life is just fine, and doesn't have to be far from true. It shows that I'm more of a stronger, cooler, smarter individual to say no and just don't do them. I wish I had picked that path in life.

My home life with my aunt and uncle was pretty rocky. My aunt tried to make things normal. My little cousin was just like a sister. My brother was always teasing her, and I was always dressing her up like a doll. My uncle and I didn't always agree on everything. We both were kind of stubborn and wanted things our own way. The arguments seemed to be getting worse and more intense. Now looking back, my brother and I did just come in to change and disrupt their whole way of life.

Where the house was located, we had water and streets to separate the houses. The inlets went out into the wild blue ocean. One of the pebble beach gang lived in the next inlet over from me. One day, he went shuffling off to visit my friend, Debbie. He walked up the stone sidewalk and knocked on the slightly opened door. As he entered, he yelled for my friend but instead he was welcomed with gruesome despair. There in front of him was my friend's father. He was hanging from the ceiling by his belt. Panicked he ran back out the open door. Debbie and I were just coming around the corner about this time. The shocked individual plowed into us full force with terror in his eyes, and stopped us from entering the awful scene. My friend screamed as he told us of his discovery. As she fell to the ground, I held her. Just like me, again, not able to say goodbye. Unless this has intimately happened to the reader, there is no explanation that I could possibly give for anyone to understand or relate to. A goodbye, or some type of closure is needed. My friend, like myself, had to put one foot in front of the other and keep going. I wish her dad had reached out, grabbed on, held steady. When you take your life, you are just thinking of yourself, a permanent way to rid the pain. Think of family who are around, no closure, and a lot of whys, and no way to turn back time. Ask for help, get help, and go on. Debbie and I talked and talked, and did one of our normal around the block walks. It would be our last one ever. When everything was said and done, she had to move in with a sister the next town over. I didn't get to see her much after that. I put my portable blue 8-track player up on my shelf, in my total black and white room. I hope I was there for her when she needed. I guess my mission with her was complete. If I look back on my life, and I have helped, guided, listened, or been there for at least one person, I have done much, and that is why I keep on. Look for the one that needs a hug, some comfort, or an "it's going to be okay."

I was fortunate to land a summer job working in the office at my school. Many applied but just two other girls and I had been chosen. It was a lot of fun, and I always had the older secretaries laughing with my jokes and unusual stories. One of the best jobs was typing every ones schedule for the fall. I made my own personal itinerary well equipped with best friends, cute guys, and great teachers. I also took part time jobs painting murals in people's houses, so I kept busy. The summer went too fast like it always does. School was to begin, so my office job there was done. Since we only attended school for half a day, I needed to find something to do the other half. I landed a job at a bank, First Jersey. It was in the data processing office. It was good money, but very monotonous. I found myself filing checks in my sleep at night.

I actually enjoyed school. I was one of the fastest typists in my class, and in the honors class for English. I loved my peaceful, enlightening art class. I never cared for any of my chorus teachers, but loved to sing. Taking photography made it easier to go to my last class, which was history. I met an interesting person in my art class. He was tall and his bangs were always covering his eyes. He spoke his thoughts out loud even if no one agreed with him, and he was an excellent artist. I was lucky enough to sit by him and hear about details going on in his life. His stories were always more risky and daring then I could involve myself with. One day he invited me over with a few other friends. He said he wanted me to meet his older brother. He thought we would hit it off. I went and we did. We became great friends. All my spare time, we spent laughing together. He worked, played keyboard, and had a brand new pickup. What more could I ask for? We went to a lot of concerts, parties and had a lot of fun together. His family was very nice and consisted of a bunch of boys. We got along great, but I think I just had too much going on. Between my life in general, school, work, teenage tension that goes along with having a boyfriend, and the edginess at home. Everything was getting to me. My uncle and I were just not getting along. So it was probably in everyone's best interest that my brother and I headed back to the big state of Ohio. We packed up what we could and flew back. It was great to see my grandparents again, but I was going to miss my family and friends I had made in New Jersey. Time to deal with change, again.

My parents getting married in Washington 1964
Carolyn & Bernie

Our humble abode, Mom and I shoveling snow. You can see the water tower I talk about in back.

My father, mother and I, born Feb. 12, 1965.

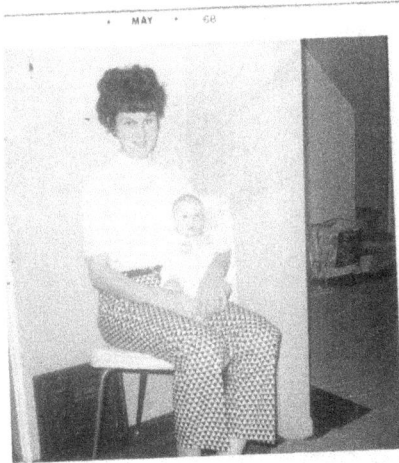

My bothersom
orother, Bryan,
oorn Feb. 22, 1968

He cut his hair
for picture!
(he-he)

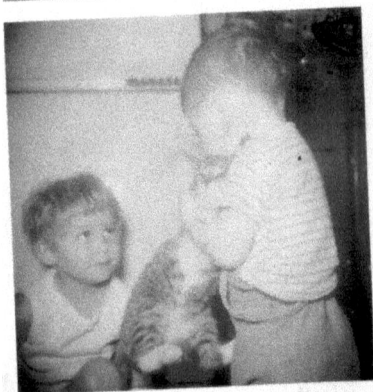

My brother "hugging" our cat.

First day of kindergarten

My favorite christmas ever! Last one before my parents divorce.

School, my ~~bage I~~ flowered book bag trimmed in black, I filed my mother's day cards & presents

My mom taught
at different schools
in the area. I
had her as a
substitute while
my teacher was
on maternity leave
in first grade.

Together right before
my mother, her ex-sister-in-law, Linda,
leave for ill-fated trip.

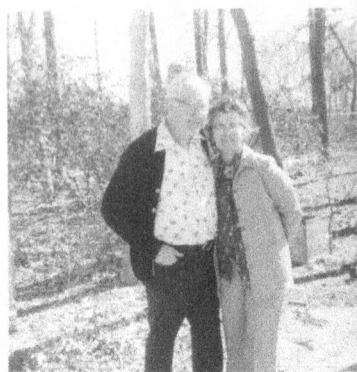

My grandparents Carroll & Florence Guindon

Their home on Harris Rd in Lodi

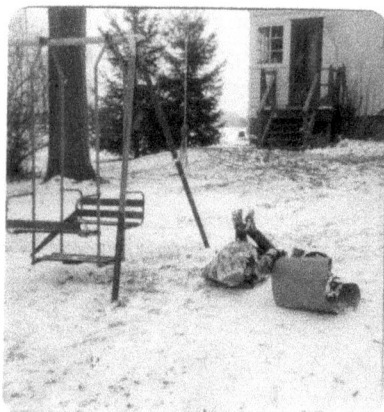

Playing in backyard at Grandma's

Playing dress-ups with neighborhoo friends

3rd Grade

Holding Flowers from mothers Funeral

My heart shaped
cake my grandmother
always made for
my birthday

My Uncle Fred, Aunt June & cousin Jennifer we moved to in New Jersey

Living in N.J.

My Cousin Jennifer and I

Was kicked out
of house in N.
So moved bac
to Ohio

My first car.

My graduation
picture

My brother, and Mikes daughter Jessica.with me

Our nice "Biker Quaker Wedding" in the woods, August 1988

Our First
Addition
Jennika Carolyn
Laird
June 1989

Our Second, Billy Michael
Oct. 5, 1990   Laird

Our Happy Family

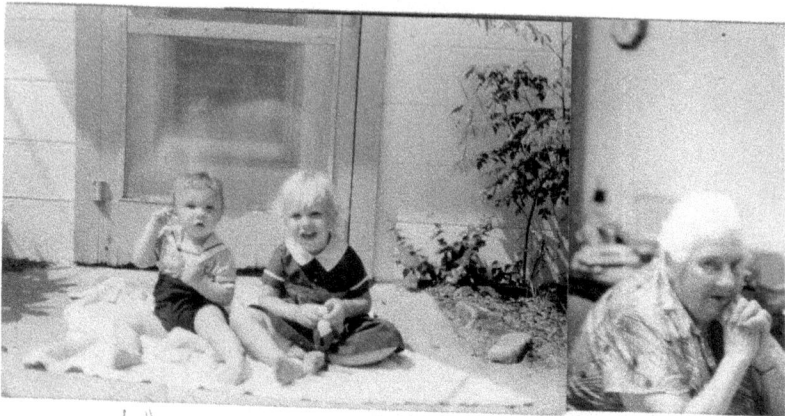

When we went to Florida for summer to take care of my Grandmother Baker, we stayed in little house in backyard.

We lived with my grandparents in Lodi, while we built our house around the corner from them.

After he was in a whole
year.

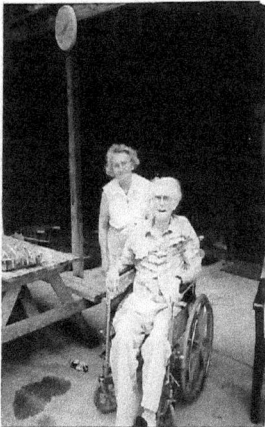

My grandfather after having
a stroke, not long before
his death.

After Mike's Death

I met Tony Helton. My husband now.

Billy, Jennika, and our dog black pug. "meatball"

Grandma; after she moved in with us with alzheimelmer's

I am loving life now
I live for helping
others. And I have a
GREAT family!

KENT STATE UNIVERSITY

This is to certify that
the Board of Trustees of Kent State University,
upon the recommendation of the Faculty, has conferred upon

CAROLYN J. BAKER

the degree of

BACHELOR OF SCIENCE IN EDUCATION

Given at Kent. Ohio, this twenty-sixth day of August,

nineteen hundred seventy-two.

PRESIDENT, BOARD OF TRUSTEES

REGISTRAR

PRESIDENT OF THE UNIVERSITY

DEAN, COLLEGE OR EDUCATION

to mom

Ohio Woma
Dies in Cras
On R. 309

A 30-year-old Lodi, Ohio, wo
an was fatally injured in a tv
car collision along Route 309
its intersection with Saucon V
ley Road north of Center Vall
this morning. A second wom
was hospitalized with injuri
sustained in the crash.

Upper Saucon Township P
lice Chief William J. Edma
Sr. identified the deceased a
Carolyn J. Baker.

He said the impact of th
crash sent the Baker vehicl
skidding along the highway
landing in a ditch at which tim
the woman was thrown from the
ripped open left side of the ve
hicle and was pinned under the
car.

The woman was dead on ar

Continued on Page 56, Column

52

my dad, brother and me

The United States of America

honors the memory of

BERNARD H. BAKER

...ificate is awarded by a grateful
...n recognition of devoted and
...consecration to the service
...untry in the Armed Forces
...United States.

Jimmy Carter

President of the United States

Sunday, February 10, 1980   Akron Beacon Journal E5

Man, 38, killed in crash

Bernard H. Baker, 38, of 9191 ...ngress Road, was killed and ...s 14-year-old daughter injured ...en their car went through a ...p sign and hit a tree, Medina ...ice said Saturday.

arrival at Medina Community Hospital. His daughter, Terri, of 8876 Harris Road, Lodi, was reported "stable" in the same hospital.

The ...

CHAPTER SEVEN
Plunging into the World of the Unknown

I was seventeen, and it was my senior year of high school. Everyone had their own things going on, people changed, and so had I. I plunged headfirst into the world of unknown and made the best of it. Something I was getting good at. At one of our high school football games, I ran into someone I had met before after moving to the small state located on the Atlantic ocean with the foreign speaking people—New Jersey. We shared our memories, and hit it off. He also had a misplaced childhood, but with different circumstances. It seems like I am a magnet for people who had a rough time growing up which is fine with me, because I love helping people in any way I can. I would like to write a book just on people having troubles in their childhood and going on with their lives in spite of it.

My boyfriend from New Jersey was still trying to make things work between us. I wasn't good at making a long distance romance work at all. He made the long trip to Ohio every other weekend. It was 500 miles one way. He'd call every day, and was always planning our future. One day he came to pick me up after school. I thought it was a nice surprise. Until I got in his car. I could see tears in his eyes. He had stopped at my house first, and pieced a letter together. The fragments were staring at him from the garbage can. I didn't remember what it had said, I just knew he wasn't happy. I had to come clean and let him know this long distance thing wasn't working, and he needed to move on with his life. I had never seen him so upset or distraught before. We talked and talked, but I was not changing my mind on how I felt. I stepped out of the vehicle and waved, as I closed another chapter of my life. I guess he didn't head for home, he went south. And kept driving and driving until he could go no further. He stayed down there until he ran out of money. His dad wired him money if he would come back and work for him, and life went on. I've talked to him a couple of times since then. His brother that was my age that I had known in my art classes had died unexpectedly. My ex-boyfriend still sounds very ambitious. He is married, doesn't have any children but has money and seems happy. I wish him the best.

I ended up getting a place with that other guy. Life was pretty much a big party, especially when I turned the eternal age of eighteen. I was still in high school when I received my parent's life insurance benefits. It was quite a bit of money, and I was definitely not prepared for it. From my very unfortunate experience, I can say at eighteen years old, I was not ready to accept a large sum of money, especially with no guidance. If anyone has some type of inheritance or insurance to leave, I strongly suggest they distinguish the age at which the money will be dispersed.

My first mission to complete was getting the car my dad had promised me. My dream car: a black Trans AM. I went to quite a few car establishments with no avail. I did find a red Trans Am though, so away I went with my craving desire. With no mechanical help or common sense. As I was driving home from school, the very next day the engine blew up. The dealership was not accommodating at all. They did not care about my situation. They did not care it was just the day prior I bought this vehicle from them. They did not care I paid cash. As I tried to convey my predicament to the employee, he just yelled at me, even cursed, when I reviewed my plight. Like it had been my own entire fault, and I did something utterly wrong. I just wanted my dream car, and I was willing to work out anything to fulfill my vision. I found out about the lemon law and had to hire a leaching lawyer just to get the dealership to acknowledge me. I had to pay a ridiculous amount of money only to have it resolved by them putting in another crappie engine. That magnificent motor lasted almost two months. Well, I had a dream a little while.

I had a lot of parties and met a lot of the wrong people. During this celebration of time I always worked, and I graduated from high school. After twenty-one graduation parties that were mandatory to validate I graduated, I went forth into college and onto a higher assembly of social gathering. By this time, I was on my fourth automobile and my funds were slowly trickling away in the wind. A pretty metallic blue Camaro off the showroom floor caught my attention. I had a very busy schedule; I worked as a preschool teacher, went to college, and partied at night. I had three different existences going on.

I've met a lot of people, good, bad and ugly. I also learned a lot of things, good, bad and ugly. Some people I have met over my lifetime have met a harder fate than me. Once in a while, I ponder about a quiet little girl I had known when I was about nine. I wondered what her fate had produced, and if she was still walking on this earth. Her parents rented a trailer nearby. I remember her being thin and frail. Her name was Tebby. She had a pale complexion with short brown blunt cut hair, and dark circles under her eyes. She always had scratches and bruises covering her fair bony legs. I remember Tebby giving me gadgets and trinkets wanting me to be her friend. She acquired many different tiny mechanical toys and huge stuffed animals. I am not sure of her father's occupation, but he would bring home boxes full of them. I just know that I disliked the yells and screams that would carry on behind closed doors while I was there. In a rage her mom or dad would grasp her up like a rag doll, and drag poor Tebby to the bedroom. Usually waving a black belt or sometimes just a fist. If I had known what set off this fury, I would have tried to be her defender. Feeling so helpless, I would sit and wait for her to emerge so I could comfort her. She would always protect her providers by different fables. When exiting the *torture chamber* she would always exclaim she had deserved the punishment, as she would beg me not to tell. We would retreat to the bathroom and bandage any war wounds while she would try to wipe away her tears. When it was time for me to go, I hated to say goodbye, but she would impress upon me, "You better hurry so you don't get in trouble." So I would run out the door and look back and wave. I could barely see Tebby's face, but her hand would be up against the window with her small fingers spread. One day as I walked over to pay a visit on my frail friend, I noticed the rusted pick-up that was always parked in the driveway was missing. I knocked on the door and got no response. I walked over to peep in. I was unable to reach it, so I went and got a plastic crate to position myself higher. To my surprise when I peered in, the place was empty. There was only a few clothes scattered, some boxes, and a few of my friends stuffed animals placed in a corner. No fragile friend in sight. They had packed up and moved on, and even though I only knew her for a short time, I was really going to miss her. I hoped things got better for her. This was one of those dysfunctional families that makes me wonder why anyone or everyone is permitted to have kids. I have other places to suggest where they can rid their pent up aggressions.

Everything that happens when a person is younger has an impact on life, big and small, good, and bad. I cannot forget, even though sometimes it is stashed way back in my memory. Before having children people need to look ahead, plan, think, make sure of readiness for such a commitment. Obviously some people were not meant to take on that responsibility. They should have purchased a pet rock or a blow up punching bag Bozo like I had when I was four.

Another case was a neighbor girl that I knew when I was younger. She would only be around in the summer while she was visiting her grandparents. I liked hanging out with her brother who was the same age as me. There wasn't much of a chance to do things on our own though. His sister seemed to have it out for me. Any chance she got, she would pick on me, and come up with vicious words and punches. I always wondered why she had so much anger toward me. As we got older the hatred started slowing down, and she would want to hang out with me more. But I had my own friends and my own dilemmas going on. After we went to New Jersey, I really never heard from her again until I had grown up (Ha-ha).

One day after I had moved back to Ohio, and was all situated into my own abode, I received a phone call from my grandmother. She stated my old volcanic neighbor and a friend were at her house asking about me. So, I headed in that direction to behold my old friend and her friend on the front porch sitting next to a cardboard box and garbage bag full of their worldly belongings. She looked about the same, but an older version. Short, sandy colored hair, and about the same height as myself. They both looked tired and ready for a shower. They had just hitchhiked up from Florida where they had lived. Our surprise reunion consisted of small talk and hugs and then an invitation back to my model existence. We all exchanged stories, then I proposed they stay over. The following morning I stepped over my comrades and shuffled off for work. When I came home that evening the house was clean, and they both informed me of their new jobs down the road. I wasn't sure how to respond or what that exactly meant, but I felt like I should be happy for them and participate in their merriment. I deciphered this must mean I have roommates even though I did not ask for any of those.

Anyway, the next day my new roommates and I went off to work. All was well. Well, for almost a day. I came home to find the house in disarray, not anything like the day prior. My old friend called to me from the kitchen. She had prepared dinner, using my food, but it's the thought that counts. (At least I have always believed in that.) I questioned where our other roommate was, and she matter-of-factly announced she departed to Florida. That was about all the information she was going to divulge. Then as we ate our meal, and she revealed that she needed to converse with me over a couple of drinks. Baffled, I went and changed clothes, and we headed out for a local pub that was full of red necks and friends to set free with. We talked and laughed, after my fourth cocktail, she asked if I knew any lesbians. Well, I stumbled back, "Not that I know of," I said. At that time, I don't even think I had even said the word, let alone knew one. If the question didn't throw me, the next statement knocked me off the bar stool. She stated that she is one, and has been in love with me, even while we were growing up. Not sure how to sincerely respond or put words together that made sense, the conversation was at a standstill. I figured it was time to go, so we got up and headed for my house.

The next day I went to work like it was just another non-chaotic day.

Only to return home to find no old friend to greet me. My quiet house seemed to leave me no clues. I walked into the kitchen to find a story on the table. This memo helped clear up the last couple of days. It went on to profess her feelings toward me as kids. While I was thinking she hated me while we were younger, maybe she just hated the feelings that she was having for me. The story unfolded about the girl with her had been her lover, and when she expressed her real intentions for the trip to Ohio, my other old roommate did not react well. Now she was headed back to try and reconcile and go on with life. It was signed: The End.

I hadn't heard anything for a while, except an occasional collect call. One day I decided to accept to see how life was treating her. She happened to be staying at a mental hospital for trying to kill herself. She talked about her brother passing on that I was a friend with. She then blurted out about wanting to come out my direction to visit. Which was fine, but I wanted her to be clear of my feelings for her, I loved her as a friend. The conversation ended, and that was the last time I heard from her.

She did leave a very big phone bill, but in the future, that was a calling card left from other roommates too. Just because I didn't have feelings for her, I did care for her as a person. I know a lot of times that she was treated unfairly. One thing I don't understand is, why all people can't just be accepted for whom they are, and be able to go on with their lives. Whether they're green, or have mauve and lavender stripes down their sides, or if big or tiny or have a peculiar habit of collecting salt and pepper shakers. That should be fine, go forth, as long as no one gets hurt. As for being gay, for most people, I believe are born that way. Everybody has their own belief, and nothing is set in stone. Why would people take on the chance of being ridiculed and choose a sometimes misunderstood fate? There are so many people walking on this earth that think they have the right to talk down others and judge others, People need to worry more about their own life and plight on this earth.

Like I was saying, over the years I have met a lot of people. Some I wish I had never had the pleasure of meeting, but it seems to all go back to making me the person I am today, stronger, and able to handle things that are dealt my way.

It was not working out with the person I was seeing, and he and I started going our own ways. He didn't want to go away, but I did. I left him all my furniture, silverware, a car, appliances, shampoo, blankets, pictures, everything, and left for my quest in life. Matthew had marriage in our future, but I couldn't see that far. I got a place of my very own in the same town. Since he wasn't prepared to move on, that probably wasn't a very good idea. In the middle of the night he would pick the lock, break the chain off and check to see if I was alone, then leave. Sometimes he'd want to converse, but I would direct him toward the door. It was a door hard to close. I look back and review the frenzied times we had. Matt let his jealousy get the best of him at times.

I remember a time he was driving my Cutlass, and I was in my Trans Am. He saw a guy friend in the car and proceeded to ram the side of our cars together. We went around the circle in town about twenty times before I was able to veer off a side street and loose him. Another time he got jealous of a biker who kept handing me quarters to put in the jukebox. It was a little hick bar in a little hick town and the biker had back up. We only had us. I could tell by Matthews red face, grinding teeth, and venomous words he was past hard boiled. I convinced him that it was past dinnertime, and we needed to vacate. We almost made it out the exit before the guy called him something like an intimidating, unattractive, unintelligent, piece of cheese. As he opened the door to step out, he turned around to be greeted with a pair of brass knuckles to his forehead. He went earthbound as the guy jumped on top of him swinging. I yelled for help as I was trying to pull the excess weight off to no avail. At least the other bikers just watched and cheered. No one jumped into make the squabble uneven. My ex grabbed a beer bottle he felt on the ground nearby and bashed the opponents head. Blood squirted as he jumped off, holding his crown. I grabbed Matt and sprinted across the parking lot. We jumped in one of my hot rods. As I peeled out, he grabbed the steering wheel and veered toward their bikes. I clenched the wheel, yanked the other direction and sped off. As I look back and critique this time, I guess I have experienced a few bar room brawls.

I think my ex-boyfriend drank so much because of his pent up aggressions and violent tendencies extending back to his troubled childhood. I have many friends that had problem pasts. He has since moved away, but returned. He came up to visit not too long ago. He has found religion, has a little girl and wanted to apologize for days gone by. Like I said before, people I have crossed paths with made me who I am today.

Anyway, needless to say, I did not have any gentlemen friends visit my new residence. For anyone who has experienced living in an apartment building, I bow to you. The people living above me must have had twenty-two kids that were half-elephant. A few times I was waiting for my ceiling to cave in. The couple on the right of me were nice, except they enjoyed heavy metal music until four in the morning. My other burden was my new neighbor, David. He was about my age and seemed calm and harmless. One thing that disturbed me about David was, whenever I looked out my sliding glass door, he seemed to be standing there, staring in. When I would take notice he would nonchalantly stroll away, or commence to knock at my door. He would always have frivolous fables to recount. I would blatantly stare into space and smile as I pretended to absorb his pointless tales. The final story was when a bad storm struck. The electric went out and my lifesaver bolted right over to check on me. I asked to use his cell phone to call my date, to let him know I would be running late. As I conferred with my companion on the phone, I noticed my narrating neighbor scrunching slowly down the couch closer to me. As I was closing the conversation, my nosey neighbor was almost sitting in my lap. As I awkwardly handed him his phone, he was rubbing my back. As he tried to lock his lips on my face, I jumped up and told him to shut my door on his way out. I ran into the rain to my get-away car, and sped off. I left behind my long flowered couch and blue chair that didn't match, my small TV, and an exercise bike. I left my bedroom consisting of a mattress on the floor and two dressers. The only thing I could not live without was my faithful music making wood grain alarm clock. I ended up moving out of there, too much headache and no privacy going on in that structure. I just needed some space. I saved up some money to rent a little house in another little town. I had enough of the apartment life. Onto my next challenge.

CHAPTER EIGHT
The Knights in Shining Armor Hanging Out in My Nightmares

My judgment was definitely blurred and misplaced. I was seeing my last ex-boyfriend's friend, and then moved on to seeing his friend's friend, Jason. I now know that I would have been doing a lot better to have just stayed by myself, on my own! The new so called friend that I ended up seeing beat me continuously. I couldn't talk to friends, be myself, or do anything right. Jason would always make some excuse to beat me. He was cautious enough to make sure he punched me in places that would not show. Never on the face. I had it instilled in my mind, I can rebuild him, change him, help him work though his problems of violence. This helping mode went on until I was able to scream, "No More," and conquer my feelings of failure again. He wasn't changing, so I moved on to the next looser, I mean knight in shining armor. Someone I stood up a few times and I wish I had kept on. Without using my brain, I stupidly decided to dive on into another senseless relationship.

First, I had to go get my belongings, and talk to the tormented soul who was threatening to kill himself, if he could not keep his punching bag that he loved. The new looser wanted to tag along, but I told him I could handle it. Well, that was an understatement. I walked into Jason's lair, the door slammed shut and locked behind me. He commenced to yell and scream obscenities at me. His presentation consisted of threatening to beat me so bad that no one would want to be with me. As I tried to present my point of view, I was pulled to the floor by my hair, and then it was yanked out. After about the third blow to my head, I don't remember much. I guess the rule of not hitting where it shows, did not apply any longer. I was down for the count. When I came to, my head was throbbing, and everything was looking fuzzy. I crawled toward the phone, only to find it was torn from the wall. As I looked out the window, I observed my car was gone. The place looked like a tornado plowed through. I held my head as I made it to the bathroom. I looked in the mirror and tried to figure how I got to this page in my life. I washed the blood off my face, and tried to brush my matted hair. My clothes were shredded, so I picked up a flannel shirt lying on the floor to put on. I cleaned up and did what I did best, went on.

When I heard my car screech into the driveway, I dashed out the back door and sprinted around the side of the house. I darted toward the car and jumped in. I locked it; then grabbed the extra key under the mat. I didn't see anyone around as I rushed out of the driveway, and never looked back. As soon as I got home, I bolted the doors and jumped in the shower. I blasted my music and tried to lose my mind in the song. Nobody deserves to be treated that way. The majority of people who hit and abuse rarely change. It's better to leave and get far away from the situation. I know people who sit in the same sad situation, thinking it will get better. They're stuck in a dream state, believing things will change. Meanwhile life is passing them by and their self-esteem, self-worth, and well-being slowly diminish into thin air. Don't get caught up in a cycle, and don't be another statistic. Be strong, go on.

During my abusive boyfriend syndrome, I was still trying to work, and go to college. I had taken all my child development courses and moved onto education classes. I went to college bars and college parties often. Amy, a girl I had met in my English class, and I went to a few social events together. A guy she liked was throwing one party in particular, and we attended. The evening started out fine, we played a drinking game called quarters. The rules were simple enough: try to bounce a quarter into a glass; make it in and pick someone to drink. Everyone was laughing, even me, until I glanced over and noticed my girlfriends dream guy was glaring at me. He started picking me to drink, drink, and drink. The room was starting to move without me and my stomach was screaming—STOP! My friend was enjoying the host, as I told her about my bothersome affliction. Amy asked her dream man to usher me to a designated area to rest and recline until further notice. He pointed down an endless hallway that seemed three miles long, and told me to go to the last door on the left. As I tottered down the corridor, I stopped myself from running into the wall and turned left. I opened the door and felt for a light switch. I turned it on to find my safe haven consisted of a mattress on the floor with some pillows and a blanket. It also had a dresser with a mirror and some clothes piled high on it. I flipped the light off and fell backwards onto the mattress. When I almost had the room stop spinning, I suddenly felt pressure and total darkness on my face! I couldn't breathe! As I tried to pull off the force, my legs were kicking and my muffled screams were going unheard. An inaudible voice was chanting wasted words, and doing things to me I did not want done. I felt weak, helpless, a puppet with no strings. It finally stopped and peeled the pillow from my face, as I gasped for air. Feeling more sick then I did before, I looked up to behold my friends infatuation kneeling over me. He got up blurting his fairy tale story of how I was leading him, and he added the hilarious statement of how could I have done that to my friend. All of this as he strolled out and slammed the door. I laid frozen to the bed, in disbelief of the revolting event and ugly words that had just occurred. When I was finally able, I raised up and gathered all my dignity. I wandered out and found my friend. As I declared the injustice that just transpired, I was ready for Amy and me to stomp out in utter disgust. My friends face looked full of doubt and skepticism, as she held onto my newest nightmare's arm. He was professing his innocence as he clenched her away into the crowd, and left me standing there. I felt so alone in a room full of people. I plowed through the bodies, made it to the door, and raced to the car before tears came pouring down my face. I got in, looked forward and drove home. I turned the radio up full throttle, as I lost myself in a song again. I stopped attending college because he was in the majority of my classes. I let his simple stare and demeaning grin bother me too much. I know I should have reported him and not let him get away with such an atrocity Because of embarrassment and shame, a lot of rapes go unreported. There are support groups, or friends or family who talk with or comfort women. Sometimes in numbers it helps to tell, give strength and move forward. No one ever needs to be alone. Don't let anyone or thing belittle, degrade, or diminish a women you may know in this kind of situation. Be strong, go on.

My new knight in shining armor. I can honestly say he never violently touched me, but he had no qualms throwing inanimate objects directly at me. Greg manipulated me at every move. He was director of my life. What I would wear, eat, and when I could take a shower. Who I could talk to, and my agenda for the day. When situations would not go his way, he broke things that meant something to me. He would cut up my clothes that I liked. He also listened in on my phone calls and followed me wherever I went. As time went on, I did not feel good about myself and looking back now it is easy to see that **he** was the culprit. If only one could stand above and look down on excerpts of one's life and see how ridiculous. Yell, "STOP IT!" My money was at its end, and my Camaro got repossessed. I was partying way too much and staying up for days at a time. Then on one glorious day, I thought my life was over, but it was really just beginning again. My manipulating knight ran off with a fifteen year old with a baby. I wailed and whimpered thinking the world was coming to an end. I had resentment toward the girl, instead I should have had joy, and thanked the girl for entering into his lousy world and taking my place in his escapades. Resentment just eats a person up and goes nowhere. Besides my life making me stronger, it made me realize that you don't need somebody else to make you be somebody. Whether I have a partner in life or not, I have found I can go on. I do go on, and I can be happy.

After all that fiasco, I was penniless, jobless, and left with a lot of bills. But I did what anyone would do who is able. I picked myself back up, got a job, a beater car, and went on with my somewhat normal life. I became friends with the landlord, who now is not with us any longer. He would let me pay rent by getting him a bottle of Wild Turkey weekly, at the local liquor store, until I was able to accumulate some cash. About a month down the road there was a knock at my door.

There standing outside my door was my old resentment. Lisa was crying, holding her baby in one arm and a garbage bag full of clothes in the other. Her parents had kicked her out of the house for dating someone that was about twenty years older than her. The tainted knight had left her and moved onto his next victim. She wondered if she could stay with me until she had gotten back on her feet. Since I was on mine, and I did mentally disturbing things like this often, I did.

We got to be good friends, she helped me, and I helped her. We laughed a lot. Laughter does help through tragedies in life. We did not have much furniture, but we had an excellent stereo. Which is about the only thing we needed besides laughter. The love and happiness kept going until one day when I left the rent money with her and a friend to give to the landlord. I was putting in extra hours at work so I could try and catch up on the bills. So when I got home I was exhausted, and I didn't pay much attention to everyone sitting around with a big bag of food from McDonalds, when I entered the door. I chitchatted, said my good nights, and headed to bed. The following day I went to work like normal, only to come home to find my place a total disaster. My favorite outfits and shoes were gone. My makeup and any items that were able to fit into a garbage bag were gone, even the box of garbage bags. I tried locating my so called friend with no success. After sitting down trying to take everything in, the landlord knocked on the door to pick up the rent.

Okay, sometimes I am too nice, and a little too trusting. I had to pack up what I had left, move out and move on. During this time, I stayed with different friends, and lived out of a medium sized box. My possessions getting smaller and smaller. One of my friends that I hung out with was small in stature with a devilish grin. Every time I would see him, I would automatically smile. I miss him, he was killed by a senseless gunshot. He let me stay with him for a while, one day during my visit, we planned a cookout. As we were starting the hotdogs and hamburgers, two guys pulled up on their Harleys.

At the time, I worked at a preschool next to a Harley dealership. When I brought the kids outside on the playground, sometimes I would talk to one of the managers next door. During my lunch, when possible, I was lucky enough to go for a ride on the new bikes. I remember him asking if I knew anybody who had a bike. I can honestly say I didn't, but it was right after that I met a whole slew of them. About a week later I rode in with about eight new friends. He must have thought I was some kind of fabricator or thought I didn't understand what a motorcycle was.

Back to the cookout, as one of them exited his bike, I couldn't help but stare. He seemed so striking, tall, with brown hair, and beautiful blue eyes. As our eyes met we could not take them off each other. Instantly we started talking. We talked for hours like we had known each other forever. He seemed real, fresh, sincere, and so different than anyone I had ever met. He told me how beautiful he thought I was, and that he had two tickets to Pink Floyd. From that day forward we were together. If you believe in love at first sight, this was definitely it. I automatically jumped onto the back of his bike, and about twelve of us rode off into the sunset.

CHAPTER NINE
The Quiet Biker Quaker Wedding in the Woods

We ended up getting a place together. It was like no past relationships I had ever had. We respected, accepted, enjoyed being with each other, had fun, and yet gave each other space to breathe. I could not ask for anything better. I was actually not spending as much time thinking and dwelling on the past. I couldn't change the past, but I could learn from my mistakes. I have yet to meet anyone perfect or who has not made any mistakes. Nor do I want to; how boring they would be. I finally was able to look forward, and get closer to fulfilling my dream. My dream of having a quote unquote *family*.

After being together for a year, we decided to get married. After our trip out to Sturgis, we came back and had a nice little quiet biker Quaker wedding in the woods. We all sat in a circle, and then we declared our love for each other. Amongst friends trying to make sure, and that they were on their best behavior, and we are still celebrating from the night prior. The lumberjack next door was cutting down trees, and some of our guests who were sitting were slowly sinking into the muddy ground, and it turned out perfect. After the regular reception, we had a little bash at our home. About thirty of us went riding around the small villages on our Harleys, blasting our horns. I was sitting on the back of my husband's 47 Knucklehead in a huge white wedding dress with my train dragging behind, wooohoooo!

My new husband had all the qualities you could conjure up and dream about as a young girl. He was smart, charming, and handsome with a sense of humor. A great provider, at times working three jobs and doing side jobs for extra cash. Always ready to lend others a hand. He was very attentive, loving, and always handing me compliments. We had a lot of the same views, and liked doing things together.

During this time in my life, I had met a lot of my good friends. Many were people who ride bikes, which at times in my life, I have heard negative

69

connotations about. The people I met would not hesitate to help you. They are more real, down to earth, and friendlier than a lot of other people I have met. It is funny, because when I look back on spring break in Daytona, while I was going to college, the guys were a lot more disrespectful, drunk, and destructive than bike week in Sturgis. I have been to Sturgis a few times and visited many bike and swap meets that were memorable times. I have attended a few races, shows, and met a lot of interesting people. Never judge a book by its cover, and I learned not to believe everything that I hear—I investigate.

About a month after we were married, I got pregnant. We were both very excited. Being pregnant was a new peculiar experience. I just wish someone had informed me about getting so big, the stretch marks, the aches, the moodiness, and every other irritating aggravation that goes on. A friend and I were pregnant at the same time. We majorly bonded, and we can relate to each other, and of course to someone else who has a big baby belly. We became very close throughout the years. Our babies ended up being one day apart. My adventures over the years with her deserve a whole book by itself. One morning during this whole enlightening affair, I woke up with a terrible backache. I thought I had slept wrong but the pain continued and was getting worse. We called the doctor, and he said to come on down. Like we were contestants on the "Price is Right." After giving me a thorough exam, he told me to go on home. He told me to relax; I still had another month to go. Wow, I get to endure the pain of someone punching me in the back for a whole month. So I called my grandparents to share in the pain. My grandmother wanted to time my irritation. After that she told my husband to call the doctor, she needs to go in. I tried to get across to everyone that I did not finish reading my library books yet. So I did not know how to have a baby. Nobody was listening, so I grabbed my bag and books. I proceeded to read about how to have a baby all the way to the hospital. It was a definitely a crash course. The hospital we had chosen was not close by either. When we finally arrived, I walked in still clasping my book. My husband scrubbed up and dressed up like a doctor. It wasn't as intimate or as personal as I thought it would be. Everyone was focusing on me with just his or her eyes revealed from behind masks, staring into an area I hadn't seen for eight months. Within minutes the baby finished popping out. It was a girl. I was so lucky, everything went perfect. They wheeled me back to my room. I jumped up, took a shower and wanted to go home. Since the baby exited a month early, they wanted us both to hang out a while longer. After they cleaned up the little bundle of joy, they brought her to me to hold. She was so very beautiful.

Within months I was "impregnated" again. I hadn't even lost my weight from the first one. At least this time around, I knew how to have a baby. Our goal was going fast forward, and I did not want anything to get in our way. After years of saving money, we were able to buy a beautiful wooded lot. It was land contract and located around the corner from my grandparents. I wanted to be close to them, so I could help them out when needed, since they had been there for me. We had to save some more money and build up some equity in the land before building a home.

This pregnancy was going into overtime. About a week after my due date, I found myself sitting in a puddle of water. I wasn't sure, but I had heard about water breaking before the painstaking event. My husband was having tires rotated on a police car he got at an auction. When I tracked him down, I could hear him yell to the mechanics to get the tires back on and he'd come back later with cigars. I waited in the front yard with my big black bag in my hand. He pulled up, I jumped in and away we flew. The baby's head was trying to exit its environment as we drove illegally in the median. When we arrived, my husband grabbed a wheelchair out of midair and wheeled me right up to our cozy room. This event wasn't as exhilarating as the last. No bright lights, extra fans, and tension in the air. This time it took place in a laid back environment set up like a family room without the pool table. I didn't even observe my husband scrub up, and he was still in his filthy attire. By the time the doctor arrived the baby was already headed out to celebrate his birthday. It was a boy. He had everything but the birthday cake. Our family was complete. Now everything will be grand.

I wish that I could proclaim times ahead were perfect and wonderful. If anyone knows, I do, that life is unpredictable. Our life was up and down. I was used to riding on a roller coaster, I just had to hold on tighter. I went back to work about a month later. Between my husband and grandparents they watched the kids. Since I had access to preschool materials, I brought them home every night and worked with the kids. At age two they could accomplish feats and concepts a kindergartner could. With children it good to start teaching and working with them at a young age. Their brain is a sponge absorbing everything that comes into its path. Not only ABCs and counting, but common sense, manners, feelings, sharing, and getting along with others. I worked with low income families who had preschool age children. I got to work with the kids along with the adults, teaching parenting skills. I also learned doing this, and loved working with people. Since the age of seventeen I have worked with young children, I have been claimed Miss Terri for many years, even by some of my friends, who I might say are children just trapped in adult bodies. My husband's two delivery jobs kept him on the road a lot. During this time we missed out on a lot of time of togetherness, and communication. Yet, as long as we kept on the same page and proceeded on with the same goals, everything would work out fine. It was pertinent we both kept working to make and save enough money to build our new dream home.

Since I was horrible in math and far from being an accountant, my husband took care of the money. He made sure all the bills were paid, the checkbook was balanced and all of that good stuff. My input was handing him my paycheck at the end of the week to deposit. Now looking back I wish I had been more involved, and had learned about budgeting and paying bills.

We managed to keep our credit immaculate. We had taken out at least five small loans, and made sure to pay them on time. We had different credit cards we had used only in emergencies. Our credit had to be perfect in order to get a home loan. After about six attempts, we finally found a bank to work with us. Our loan was approved and was in the process of going through. Hurray! Of course things were going a little too well, so I'm always ready to brace myself for whatever might come my way.

Not too long after the bank approval, we started receiving phone calls from bill collectors. I asked my husband about these late payment inquiries we were receiving. My husband had a way of saying the right thing, comforting me and easing any fears that might be running around in my brain. He informed me there must be some kind of mistake. I accepted that, but the calls and letters kept coming and getting more threatening. While my husband was just shrugging them off, I started to do some investigating myself. I would never cut it as a detective, though, I can't even tell you what someone was wearing the day prior, let alone myself. I was discovering matters I could not comprehend. While searching through paperwork and making phone calls, I unearthed credit cards I did not know existed. All of them maxed out and over the limit. There were Visas, MasterCards, Discover cards, gas cards, store cards and two loans I knew nothing about. Even my own Visa and Discover card that I had only used one time in my life were over their limit. I had only used my Visa once and that was to get the kids Mickey Mouse curtains and matching bedspreads that were half price. My mind was on a temporary overload. Gaskets were blowing I didn't even know I had. I was clueless on what could possibly be going on. With bills in hand and questions ready to shoot out of my mouth, I sat and waited for his arrival. The homecoming was taking too long, so I decided to go out myself to get some answers. I ventured out hoping to vanquish my curiosity thoughts and theories. His tight lipped friends gave no answers or comforting antidotes. I could not find my husband, so I drove around organizing my speech. Whatever was going on, I was ready to put my foot down and everything else I needed to, because it looked like everything was crumbling fast. I was so in love with my husband, and I believed in him and everything he said. I try to believe in everyone and always want to think the best of people.

When I arrived home, his van was in the driveway. He was upstairs playing with the children, carrying on like normal, and looking normal. What could possibly be going on? With my paper proof in hand I confronted him. I made sure to express no more lies or lame excuses. I wanted the truth or I was going for a long walk. We went into the bedroom for our conference. He looked down at the floor as he confessed he was addicted to shooting pills, and smoking crack. As he looked up tears were in his eyes, and he asserted how sorry he was to me and the kids. We talked and talked and decided we could work through this together, on our own. I know so many couples that would throw their arms in the air instantly and call it quits. It is so easy to end a relationship and walk away without even trying, attempting different avenues together. I realize in some situations that is not an option, but a lot of times, I think we give up too easily.

We didn't tell the relatives, and I thought everything would be just fine. He said he would quit and so I thought that's that. Someone addicted to drugs rarely speaks up and declares they have a problem on their own. Sometimes it takes a drastic event. Others around will have to do what they can to make rehabilitation happen and then work, and that is not easy. It's hard when it is a child, but I feel even harder if I am talking about an adult. Their strong will, age, and denial work against getting help. I worked on trying to keep everything and myself together while keeping a watchful eye on him. I had to make our life look and seem normal. I took over the checkbook and payments. I paid a little here, a little there and tried to make everyone happy. I was still trying to fully grasp and understand everything. Like I have expressed, I am no angel, but I always prioritized, scrutinized, and took care of what I needed before I ever thought of myself.

I am very thankful our home building loan went through before our credit report was in shambles. The building of our new home commenced. Which also meant added work and deadlines to be met. Looking back, a lot of things become clearer. Like in the building of our dream home, items would come up missing, like the front door. Which would put the job behind and hold up whatever step we were on. I found myself alone through most of the decision making and deadlines that needed to be done. My husband spent the allowance money that was to be used for our home, so I just had to make do. His father got some paint for me, and I ended up doing almost all of the painting myself. A friend did the ceilings. I had to put used carpeting down before they came in to put the base boards up. This was a stressful time, but I kept looking toward the future, and the hope it would soon get better.

CHAPTER TEN
Am I Going Crazy or the Standard Insane?

Moving into our new home was going to be a new beginning. I thought it was going to feel like biting into a York Peppermint Patty. Instead of wearing a long flowing white gown and running through the poppy field, I was busy picking my husband up from jails, hospitals, dark alleys, back woods and police departments. Over the next few years, I would be taking him to rehab centers, methadone clinics, court appearances, support groups and probation appointments. I'm not complaining. I loved him and planned on sticking by him. I just couldn't comprehend the hold the drug had on my husband. Anyone who has been addicted or knows someone that is, we had good days and bad days. Sometimes good weeks, but we had to take one day at a time. Having someone in my life addicted to drugs takes its toll on the relationship, the love, and any kind of "normalcy". Our life was really high or really low. Over time I would leave him, kick him out, threaten divorce, go out with others, whatever idea I could come up with to try and stop the roller coaster. I wanted to help, but I had to set boundaries and limits. Not only for him, but myself. I tried any and every option. I didn't keep doing everything for him; I'd let him fall; and take the consequences. I tried to motivate him to get help, and keep reminding him about his good qualities. When he did not accept my help, it tested my sanity. I wish I would have went to counseling or joined a support group. In life look, ask, get help when needed. I remember at one time even telling him I wish the other substance was a woman, for then I might understand everything a little better. I would just want him to be happy, and I would have to work on myself to release him, and go on. To anyone who cannot relate or understand people who do or are addicted to drugs, they are still people. Great people who can live halfway normal lives. Even though our relationship was rough, my husband was an excellent father, even with him living with his awful disease, he spent a lot of evenings with his children playing games, helping with homework, and reading stories. The kids idolized their dad and well they should, he was an excellent person. There was only two times we raised our voices in front of the kids. After that, we didn't spend much time together because we refused to do that to the kids. Since he had been using the drug for such a long period of time it acted like a stimulant, and he was able to carry on a normal daily routine. That is why my relatives and I had a hard time believing he had a drug problem.

One thing I would do to keep my sanity and relieve tension was to visit a girlfriend, and I would personally decorate friends' homes or vehicles. I would help when it was someone's birthday or if they were going through a hard time. I would get around fifty helium balloons, bags of confetti, and one-hundred regular balloons that we would blow up on the way to our destination. I am sure we looked a sight, especially when we would do our Chinese fire drills when one of us would be out of air. We would only lose a small amount of balloons as we exited the vehicle and ran. We would attack when no one was around. We would stash balloons in the fridge, on the toilet, cupboards, the shower, under the comforter on the bed, wherever possible. The same with the confetti, inside pillowcases, pockets, socks, between towels, drawers, under the sheets, in shoes, wherever our imagination led us. I had a friend call and say that he put on one of his jackets that he had not worn in years, and there was a little reminder of me in the pockets—confetti. Then, if they were a really good friend, we would make the entire inside of their house or car a spider web, using yarn. No one, could even enter the monstrosity without a pair of scissors handy. I love to make people smile. Everyone needs some form of release, happiness, or time for themselves, whether it is reading, screaming in a corn field, making snow angels at midnight, going out with friends, watching a good movie, or shopping. We all need something to strive and look forward to. Whatever it might be, make sure to put it in a daily, or at least, weekly schedules.

Meanwhile mentally and financially, I kept things together, but the drug was just too strong for him to stay away for very long. Objects were coming up missing around the house. Bills were piling up more, and it was getting harder to keep the collectors happy and off our backs. They would telephone me daily to converse, and it wasn't to discuss the weather or my pain. They just were not sympathetic with my plight. People didn't want to hear my tragic tale. They just wanted my currency. After a while, I never picked up my phone, and I blocked out the ringing irritation. My husband, who I am sure was tired of my constant complaining came up with an idea to relieve our financial burdens. Something I never wanted to do in my lifetime— file bankruptcy.

I went ahead and set up an appointment with a financial adviser. His advice was not what I was hoping to hear. It was in our best interest for us both to claim the inevitable B word. With the high interest rates and late fees on the credit cards, I would be paying for life, even if they accepted my first born, my second born, or my tenth. He suggested a way we could do it and keep the house. Between the loans and fourteen credit cards, there really was no choice involved. We got a lawyer and made it through the whole sad, messy ordeal.

Back on the home front, I was still trying to monitor my husbands every move, which was hard with his delivery jobs. It seemed like a hopeless, vicious cycle. Sometimes his boss could not contact him, and I would have to do local deliveries up to Cleveland or over to Akron. I would load up the two car seats, pick up the packages and the kids, and I would do our bonding time. Going over colors, singing songs, and talking about our day. I felt like I was running in the same spot going nowhere in helping my husband. He was in and out of jail. Bigger, more expensive objects would come up missing. I tried many options, even shaking him and yelling "STOP!" My checks, my jewelry, money, cars, anything that was worth anything, even if it was nailed down, was gone. I had to sleep every night with my purse under my head. One day I went into the garage to get a tool or duck tape. Looking around I did not see his pride and joy, his motorcycle. When he came home, I attentively asked where it was. He acted unconcerned and responded it was in the shop. I knew this couldn't be true. He knew all about bikes. He did everything on his bike, from the motor, to the paint job, to making his own fenders. He had a fiberglass shop with his father, and he made motorcycle parts on the side. His 47 Knucklehead was a basket case when he got it. He was always helping others with their bikes too. Later I found out from someone that he sold his Knuckle for next to nothing, and of course, somebody jumped on that. I also got the blow he had moved onto heroin.

The only phone calls I seemed to receive were from bill collectors and bad news. One night there came a phone call from a hospital in Youngstown. They asked me to come pick up my husband. They wouldn't really reveal much, but I knew he hated hospitals. I took the kids to my grandmothers, and started on my quest, not even knowing where Youngstown was located. I did know it was east and almost in Pennsylvania. As long as the vehicle I am driving has a radio in it, I could drive to Antarctica. A radio also comes in handy if the car is making an unfamiliar noise. A few hours later in the overwhelming darkness, I spotted it. I ran into the emergency room doors, stated my name, and they took me to the poor, pitiful, human mass laying on the bed. He had rammed into the back of a semi. I sat down and cried, feeling like I had been at the end of my rope a thousand times. Only knowing I better just stand up and keep climbing. I had to pick him up before, but the other times he was coherent. He was kept under observation. A couple hours, and later he came to. He was very lucky, a broken arm, some broken ribs, and stitches to fix his head. When he was finally good to go, he stood up, and collapsed right to the floor. They forced him to stay as long as they possibly could, but he wanted out. As soon as he could stand, he stormed out, and we quietly wandered the roads back to our unstable home. The accident was blamed on a plate of leftovers I had sent with him. He said he had bent down to take a bite, and took his eyes off the road for a second. I knew better. We pulled into our driveway early the next morning and entered our castle, smack dab right back into the middle of our fairy tale.

He lost his driver's license, his job, and my sanity. None of that, slew the dragon. The knight got back on his trusty steed and started hauling scrap metal. It must all be coincidental that his seedy friends lived by the places he would cash the metal in at. Cleveland was his playground. He knew every nook and cranny. He was raised there. The times I would go to that foreign country to look for him, if I felt brave enough to take on such an assignment, I would get lost. The houses all look the same. It's ironic because when Cleveland friends would come down to visit, they would clamor about getting lost because all the cornfields looked the same. I have many terrifying tales of my car being stolen, a gun held to my head, being held up, being shot at, and a few other stories while trying to apprehend my best friend from his evil villains. The drug had such a tremendous hold on him. I loved and cared for him so much. Even though we lived in the same household, I missed him deeply. Trouble was engulfing him. He got caught a few times for trespassing at factories and taking scrap metal out of their dumpsters. Which some would act like he stole the king's jewels. The police came more than once to search the premises, which I had no problem with. Then it all came to a screeching halt, and he pushed his luck too far. He was sent away for a full year to prison. Of course, we would all miss him. I just dreamed this time away would clean out his system and the drug would be conquered. I felt like I might have some time to work on myself and breathe again. It definitely took its toll on the kids. They made pictures and cards for him. They missed their hero. I missed my best friend. I loved him, but hated him. If anyone has had a loved one in prison, they know how it is, especially if it pertains to drugs. While he was away, I had to let him know about his friend, that he hung out with all the time. He also was addicted to drugs, he overdosed and died. I hoped he would take this to heart and crash it into his brain.

We had different problems arise during his departure, but my life isn't normal unless chaos is stirring. My grandfather had a stroke, and my grandmother was doing everything for him. As strong willed as she was, she did not want extra help. The year of my husband's departure went fast to me. I'm sure it was slow motion for him. While he was away, I read books about heroin and addicting personalities. I jotted down any signs that I had picked up on of him using drugs. One book stated to watch any type of change in eating habits and his appearance. He hardly ate at all and did not care anything about his appearance. I had a regular routine of checking for needle marks on his arms, inside the elbow. I wouldn't let him wear long sleeve shirts. So it didn't take long before he would find new areas to shoot up. Areas to check would be between the fingers and toes, on the bottom of the feet and there are many other spots drug users use and come up with. The person's attitude changes, and they lose interest in things that were important before. Paying attention and remembering events decreases. My husband always seemed to be on the defense, and easily spilled out stories and excuses. Some people will lack motivation, and have an uncaring attitude. I watched for unexplained moodiness or nervousness combined with other signs. My husband had a habit of nodding off often. I thought it was because he was very tired, I found out later it was because of the heroin. He also had a habit of wiping his face or arms, which I found out later that he felt like he had spider webs on him, and he was trying to get them off. His pupils were constricted. He had many stashes for his poison. Inside light switch covers, in the basement rafters, inside socks, and the inside pockets of suit jackets. The majority of the time it was secretly hidden in our vast three and a half car garage. Not that he ever had any type of drug for a period of time. It was senselessly used immediately, and until it was gone.

The day arrived for his release. I drove about four hours away to pick him up. One subject that I dwell on is why some people are thrown in prison for drug related crimes. I think there would be more successful recovery rates and less recurrent crimes if the actual problem were dealt with—drug addiction. Why can't they be thrown into a drug rehabilitation clinic for a year instead, or be forced into a drug treatment program while their bodies are sitting in a cage? While in prison, instead of learning on how to beat drug addiction, people get to learn easier means of ripping people off, faster ways of getting money illegally and any other scams carelessly shared from inmate to inmate.

Anyway, on the way back from our journey, excitement filled the air. For the first time in years we articulated, we verbalized, we listened. We exchanged stories from being written up for bringing an apple to his cell, and from not knowing how to react from being treated like a caged animal for a full year. I told him about the happenings at home and then expressed concerns for the future. After talking the entire trip, the final decision was decided for us all to go back and get acquainted for a week. Then he would go stay with his brother. It would be far enough to keep him away from what so-called friends he had left. The kids would stay with him every other weekend, and we would work on our relationship. For my sanity, I did not want him back into the home until he could prove he was clean. We often did family things together, and things seemed to be going good. I'm one of those people who believe one can work out anything and until death do us part. My dream of having peace, being a family was so close. I could visualize it right in front of me. Of course when things are going too right, it usually means that something will occur. One night I received a phone call. An anonymous voice blurted out, "We can't wake him up," the unfamiliar voice trembled. I stammered back, "Who?" The voice rattled out my husband's name. I was half-asleep and not able to comprehend what he was saying. I told the voice he lived with his brother. He then uttered, "He's in the back seat." Still not revealing who he was, he then relayed the same message, "We can't wake him up." Not sure of all the circumstances I told the frightened voice to take him straight to the hospital. He wouldn't. The voice was scared. I finally convinced him to call my husband's brother. I was hoping he could persuade the shaken voice to do something. Thank goodness he was successful in getting them to drop him off at the emergency room door, and leave. I guess his concerning friends didn't want to be involved. My lifesaving brother- in-law was headed for the hospital, and he would let me know what was going on. My heart dropped to my stomach, it spends a lot of time there. I stared at the phone waiting for another call of gloom and despair. It finally rang, my brother-in-law relayed my husband had overdosed. He did die, but the doctors were able to bring him back to life. They did not have any idea what his condition would be. I took the kids to my grandparents and rushed to the hospital. When I arrived, he was conscious and was strapped down to the table. As much as he loves hospitals, he was yelling and screaming he wanted the heck out of there. I was in a fog as the doctors went over details with me and told me how lucky he was. So many things were surging through my mind. Obviously the ugly monster veered his head again and was determined not to leave my husband's life or mine. He wasn't making it easy for anyone, and he had to stay for observation. I stayed with him, trying to understand his story. It did not take me long before I realized why the doctors made him stay.

At first, I thought it was just a joke. He kept asking the same question over and over and over. He kept stating the same sentence over and over and over. I took the nurse to the side and asked her what was going on. She responded with, his short-term memory could be temporary or permanently damaged. Not being able to take this all in, I just went back over near him and plopped down on a chair. I just couldn't help but stare at this person that made me believe in love at first sight. Well, they finally released him, and the observation was done. The verdict was in; his short term memory was permanently damaged. Definitely not sure of the future, we picked up the kids and stayed together the rest of the weekend. When Sunday evening arrived, we drove him back to his brothers. What else could we all do but be strong and go on.

CHAPTER ELEVEN
My Hardest Obstacle to Overcome

He attempted work and some kind of normalcy. I can't imagine how difficult it was for him. At one time, he was such a go-getter, full throttle, ready for adventure. This set back was hard on everyone. This mundane, aggravating, lonely time went on until I thought it was time for us to try, and for him to come home. His brother deserved his own life back, and he had helped so much. The kids missed him, and so did I. Even though I knew our relationship or the person I fell in love with would never be the same. Taking on this quandary, I knew might even be more stressful then before. I would have to make sure he stayed away from bad influences, and help him remember basic things. So he moved back in with his duffel bag of clothes, and the hope things would be better. It did not take long to see he sometimes would get frustrated with himself, and I felt bad that I would get frustrated answering the same question over and over. We slowly but surely got to the point we did not talk much. I was hoping happiness would come creeping up anytime. No one involved with someone addicted to any type of substance, ever gives up. Sometimes I pace myself or take time out for myself, but never give up, and with any stressful event seek help when needed. I got him a job close by and gave him a small notebook to write things down to help him remember. I told him to write down what his boss wanted done for the day, then cross out when done. We tried to be a happy, somewhat normal family.

My grand grandmother who is such an influential figure in my life, was still trying to take care of my grandfather during all my escapades. I tried to stop in or at least call daily to see if she needed anything. My grandfather was unable to do anything himself. My grandmother, while in her eighties, got him in and out of bed, bathed him, got him in and out of his wheelchair, dressed him, everything, every day. My brother and my uncle, who is my grandparent's only son, lived there too. They helped when possible. He was in and out of the hospital. Through all of this, my grandmother kept on with her strength, courage, and stamina. I learned all these qualities from her, and more. One of the times he was in the hospital, I received a phone call. It was late in the evening but the hospital urged me to bring my grandmother right away. I drove to her home. I woke her up and told her to quickly dress, we needed to get to the hospital. We sped to the emergency room and raced to my grandfather's room. My grandmother went in, sat on the edge of the bed and held my grandfathers hand. I stopped a nurse, only to find out he had passed on minutes before we arrived. I felt so sorrowful that we did not make it in time. I felt his presence as we said our goodbyes. He was a super person. We all miss him very much. The last few years he was unable to talk and just wasn't his opinionated self. I cried at his funeral (something I don't do often) the tears kept cascading down my face.

My grandmother marched on, if I thought my mother was Superwoman's sidekick, but my grandmother must have been Superwoman herself, or maybe even Superwoman's boss. Nothing could stop her or slow her down, even with her hip replacement surgery on both sides. I remember one time she climbed up in a tree to fix her clothesline, only to have a limb break and she fell to the ground. She hurt her arm and broke a few ribs. She just got up, strolled into the house and wrapped a bandage around and around her torso and made a homemade sling. Advising me the following day when I found out about it, a doctor cannot do much for broken ribs. Not to long after this adventure, she was tossing food scraps out back, down the steep ravine. She noticed something shiny had dropped out of the bucket, a spoon. She bent down to pick it up only to stumble and tumble down the great divide! She climbed and made it up the vertical cliff and kept crawling toward the house. She crept up the stairs and into the bathroom where she cleaned up her cuts and bandaged up her ankle, she badly sprang. I would not have even known of these events if the cuts and bruises were I had not been present. She is the type of person that never wants others to worry and she never complains of aches and pains. This all from a lady in her eighties. She grew up in the depression, so she keeps about everything. Every bread wrapper (which she needs because she bakes her own bread), piece of tin foil or saran wrap, every rubber band or paper clip, any type of bag, lid or container, boxes, every piece of material, wrapping paper and ribbon or any other item that can be stashed or stored away for later use. I have inherited from her part of this trait too. I have learned to make do with what I have. Sometimes that involves duck tape and super glue.

A lot of paperwork had to be taken care of after my grandfather passed on. One of the trips back from filling out social security papers, a car made a left hand turn directly in front of my grandmother. There was no stop sign or traffic light, just straight road. My grandmother rammed the vehicle that turned abruptly into her path. My grandmother was life flight to Metro Hospital. She was very lucky to be alive. She had a few broken bones but with her strong will that would be nothing. The lady who made the turn in front of her was killed instantly.

My grandmother was going to be laid up for a while, so I got a hospital bed, changed our bedroom around and had her move in, when she was released from the hospital. My husband and I fixed a room up downstairs for us. I had no problem with this, good health or bad, I would be there for her. I think it is ironic how many people ignore their parents or grandparents or not spend the time they should with them. This is the time they need it, when they are older. They might not want to ask so that they don't feel like a burden. But *of course* there are many things they are not able to do. If an older adult does not have a son or daughter, why not a neighbor, a friend, or someone who does not have any parents or grandparents. Some say, "If I had parents, I would do whatever I could, whenever I could. I'm just not fortunate to ever get to take on this responsibility or rewarding obligation." I hope that I have instilled this belief into my children. If a person doesn't die young, they get old and need care.

This was a very busy time in my life. I took care of my grandmother, my two kids, my husband and other people's kids. There was no time for myself, but with all the commotion I never had time to think about it. One day after taking one of the kids home that I watched, I stopped at the store to pick up something for dinner. I arrived home and walked into the house ready to plop. I knew my day wasn't over, so I didn't dare sit down. I checked on my grandmother, and was happy to hear the shower on in the bathroom. I was worried because my husband was late getting home from work. I went into the kitchen to start dinner. After I got everything organized, the shower was still going. I knocked on the door to let my husband know dinner was almost ready. I got no response. I knocked louder, and yelled for him, with no response. The door was locked. I got out the trusty butter knife, unlocked the door, but still could not enter. It felt like some force was pressing against it. I kept pushing until I was able to open it a crack to squeeze through. I was waiting for someone to wake me up, because this had to be a bad dream. I must have been stuck in somebody's nightmare. Please somebody come and shake me. Through the misty fog, I could see my best friend lying on the floor. The person I stuck by and he stuck by me through thick and thin. The person, no matter what happened to our relationship, we were going to sit in rocking chairs together and reminisce about the hard times, the good times, listen to music, laugh, and get old.

My knees went to the ground. As I shook him to wake up, I told him that he was going to have to go live with his mom and get off drugs for good. I could not take this anymore. I felt his pulse. There was nothing. My heart dropped way past my stomach this time, never to return. I ran to my grandmother's side and cried about my husband not waking up. I made my son stay with her. My daughter was at a ball game with friends. I dashed to the phone, and dialed 911. Still in shock I revealed the awful scenario to the operator. My husband was not breathing.

I've had to deal with many things in my life, but right now I was dealing with the hardest. Even though my best friend was lifeless on the floor, the 911 operator announced that I needed to perform CPR on my motionless mate. The operator talked me through it, I was numb. I felt like a robot completing the commands she urged, but I really wasn't there. I kept this up until 911 arrived; they ran up the steps and took over. I was staring into a bad dream. As they worked on my best friend, the officers shot different questions at me. Some necessary, some ridiculous, but I answered best thatI could in my zombie state. I wondered how many times their best friend, soul mate of ten years, parent of their children had been lying dead next to them. Compassion wasn't in their vocabulary, it was just business, just the facts mam. No one was able to bring my loved one back. They rushed him off to the hospital, only to pronounce him dead.

The only thing I was left with was a ton of bills, no life insurance and complete sadness. Just total emptiness and the wanting of some kind of goodbye. After a lengthy investigation, they checked *undetermined* on the death certificate. I do not know for sure what happened, but have a pretty good idea. The next few days I don't remember much. Again my legs were moving forward on their own in the dark. I had to tell the kids this time their dad was never coming home. Despite the drugs, this person would do anything for anybody. Despite the disease this person was kind and more human than a lot of people who travel this earth. I am so thankful I had a chance to meet him and spend time with him. I just wish that anyone who is contemplating using drugs, would think twice before trying and using them. Anyone might end up being one of the unfortunate, or just a statistic, and leaving behind a lot of people who loved them. Please think.

Time has passed since my husband's death, and time does aid in healing. Of course, I miss him dearly and think often of our good times. Sometimes I have to take a second glance when I think I see him cruise by on his Harley. I know in time I will see him again.

Right now I have so much to do. I have many more friends to make and people to help.

I am married to my best friend and enjoying life. Both of my kids are grown, graduated from college, and are incredible adults.

I jotted down some of my experiences for others to see that everyone has problems and dilemmas. Sometimes it helps to know others who have been there, done that and moved forward. Life will get better, think positive. With inner-strength, humor, and determination anyone can break through obstacles. Each problem that I was confronted with made me stronger and the person I am today. Writing this book has also helped put needed closure in my life. Be strong and move past your difficult hurdles in life and continue your journey.

CHAPTER TWELVE
My Letter to Others

My hope in writing this book is to help others go on regardless of what their situation is. Tomorrow is another day. When I was younger, if I could have met or have known there were actually other kids out there with no mom or no dad, it would have been easier to wake up each day. Talk about death, prepare other children, help in the healing process, and in moving forward. When my parents divorced, someone could have told me it wasn't my fault and what a divorce actually meant, and it sadly happens all the time. Start young with teaching moral values, kind words and being nice to others. Talk about good touching and bad, and realize that it isn't always a stranger doing the touching. It's okay to tell, and to say, "NO." Listen to the voice prodding in the mind, and take advice from others who have been there. Understand the consequences that might occur with mixing drinking and driving. Slow down while driving, and in every aspect in life. I want to tell children to hug their parents more, and tell them that they are loved. Spend time with them. Parents do the same with offspring. Never take anyone for granted. If someone could have shouted the dangers of drugs, and reviewed all the friends I would lose to drugs, maybe I would have stayed away from them, and helped others more. Nothing good comes from drugs. You're a much better and smarter person if you're able to stay far from them. Reach out to others, even if it's just a "Hi." Talk to others when you have problems, and be a good listener when needed. I wish someone shared with me that I was somebody, and you don't need anybody else to be somebody. Don't put up with any kind or type of mental or physical abuse. There is no excuse. You are too good. Don't let anyone belittle, degrade, or diminish your will and inner-self. Get rid of resentment. Find forgiveness. Nobody is better than anyone else. Never give up. Respect and accept others and things that cannot be changed. Be supportive and a strength for those who need it. Say, "I love you," often. Laugh! Especially at the problems and worries that most likely won't happen or eventually time will help heal. Remember if you don't die young, you get old. So, help older family and friends when they need it. Be a good example for generations to come. Most of all show the people around how much you care about them, because: LIFE IS TOO SHORT!

www.ingramcontent.com/pod-product-compliance
Lightning Source LLC
Chambersburg PA
CBHW072008060426